The Young Woman
Who Lived in a Shoe

The Young Woman Who Lived in a Shoe

Elizabeth Braund

PRISCA

A Division of
Pickering & Inglis Ltd

Copyright © 1984 Elizabeth Braund

First published 1984
by Pickering & Inglis,
3 Beggarwood Lane,
Basingstoke, Hants RG23 7LP,
United Kingdom

ISBN 0 7208 0569 4

Printed and bound in Great Britain by
Hunt Barnard Printing Ltd., Aylesbury, Bucks.

Contents

Foreword to *PRISCA*

We live in an age of increasing perplexity for the
Christian woman. The Women's Liberation Movement
itself is varying in its mood, swinging from extreme
stridency, (often with lesbian overtones), to an anxiety
that perhaps it has gone too far and that women are
actually losing out as a result. The Christian Church, on
the other hand, is also uncertain in its approach, and
this is true not only in the wider oecumenical context,
but in evangelical circles also. These can show deeply
different attitudes. An article was published in a leading
evangelical magazine which maintained that to forbid a
woman to preach was unscriptural and un-Christlike,
whereas a sermon in a New York church taught that a
woman should never be allowed to handle her own
money, but should hand it over to her husband because
he was her head.

In the light of this it is obviously important for
Christian women not to be cowed by these pressures,
but to think their whole position through, honestly and
biblically. I believe that a good way of doing that is for
women to discuss these things together, and of course
one of the best means for this is the reading of books.

In the secular world, many women's presses have
sprung to life, again reflecting the various organisations
from which they have come. One of these is the *Virago*
Press, whose object it is to provide an outlet to the
writings of women both past and present, and to cover a
wide range of subjects (judicious selection is called for
on the part of the reader!).

It is my hope that the PRISCA series can achieve a similar aim, and that it should be an imprint which will publish books by or about Christian women. I would not want it to be felt, however, that all *Prisca* books must be about specifically 'women's' subjects – home-maker or career woman, bringing up children, etc. – though these may well be covered. Neither, let me hasten to add, is this a kind of 'Christian Women's Lib' series! The name PRISCA was chosen because the New Testament Priscilla illustrates best how the women in the Bible lived full and varied lives. She seems to have combined technical skills, hospitality, doctrinal clarity and counselling wisdom, and all this with the obvious love and respect of the Apostle Paul. We do not need Women's Lib to tell us that women have always made a big contribution which, we hope, will be highlighted by this series.

What I really want, therefore, is for the PRISCA series to be an outlet for women to write books about anything that interests them, whether it involves their own lives, their thinking, other people or the world around them – anything in fact that inspires them to put pen to paper! It will be good, therefore, if this series encourages new writers as well as those who have already been published, while we hope also to republish some of the 'Golden Oldies' of the past.

The Christian Church has had its Freya Starks too, women who have travelled and adventured for the Gospel; while other women wrote books which have long been out of print and forgotten, and such works may be of great value to us today.

Above all it is my desire that God may be glorified in such a series, and that we Christian women may be encouraged as we strive to fill our God-given place in society, to use our talents, and to 'adorn the doctrine' of our Saviour in everything.

Preface

I have known Elizabeth Braund for many years now, since the days when she first joined Westminster Chapel. I used to read the *Evangelical Magazine* of which she was the managing editor, and was always stimulated by its blend of sound theology and the awareness that evangelical Christians must understand, and be involved in, the secular society around them.

As those who read this book will realise, Elizabeth accepts nothing at face value. Her excellent mind and her capacity for penetrating to the root of a problem stood her in good stead when she wrestled in the magazine with questions of faith and life. But those qualities were to be of even greater value when she found herself led by God into an amazing work amongst the young people of South London.

For some years, many people have been encouraging her to write her story, which she has been reluctant to do partly because she was anxious about publicising the people whose lives she had shared, and partly because she did not feel that the time was right. So I count it a real privilege that Elizabeth has now consented to launch the *Prisca Press* with this story of God's work in her own life and in the foundation of *Providence House*.

And what a great story it is! It tells about a woman who, after becoming a Christian, was involved in Christian journalism, which was just up her street. Then she found herself almost catapulted into a job which she would never have imagined in her wildest dreams.

Those of us who have known her over the years have been impressed, not only by the qualities already referred to, but also by her wisdom, and her almost intuitive sense of how to behave in complex situations. We have been challenged by her healthy refusal to accept evangelical clichés, or customs which she has shown to be traditional rather than Christian; and we have been stirred by her understanding of, and ready identification with, the people who live around her. She has also resolutely refused to approach her work from a party political position, preferring to appeal to politicians of all shades, whether local or national, and to the police as well when she feels that there has been injustice of any kind.

Her fellow workers, too, have been vital to the work, with their love and loyalty to Elizabeth and to the young people, and it is good that they have a share in this book. But above all, such a story glorifies the God who made it all possible, and who by his grace used this faithful woman and her friends, not only to bring encouragement and order into countless young lives, but even more to bring them and their families to a knowledge of their Saviour Jesus Christ.

Introduction:
The Prospect of a City

'The McIvers are coming!'

The words rang through the crowded building like a Highland battle cry. And their effect was not dissimilar. Chatter and laughter died away. Games came to a halt. Heads turned apprehensively towards the main doors. Alarm, almost consternation, showed in the faces of some eighty youngsters.

Hoping to defuse the situation I asked casually: 'Who are the McIvers? I don't know them'. It was no good. Several muttered, 'You'll see', and 'You'll soon wish yer didn't know 'em'. But the general tension in the atmosphere remained, although after a while when nothing unusual had happened desultory talk and some games resumed.

Suddenly I was aware that these had ceased. I turned to the main doorway. It had been kicked open, and through it marched three undersized boys, the oldest of whom was barely fifteen. They evidently knew all about gangster films. Their hands were on their hips; their faces expressionless, their eyes blank and staring.

It should have been a ridiculous, laughable scene. But it was not. How could such little lads have terrorised youngsters throughout the neighbourhood? For there was no doubt that they had been doing that. What lay behind those blank faces and staring eyes?

We were to find out over the next years as slowly the McIvers shed their terrible defences, and dared to become individuals – Ron, Peter, Albert, and a fourth, the youngest, who initially copied big brothers in everything and who played in one of our football teams for a year before we realised that 'he' was in fact a girl.

All that took place nearly twenty years ago in the neighbourhood lying behind what was reputed to be 'one of the world's busiest railway junctions' – Clapham Junction in South London. At the time the area consisted of a maze of little streets of two-storeyed terrace houses, still punctuated by bombed-out spaces. There were pubs on the corners of several roads, an off-licence and a shop on others. Not far away were dim caverns under the railway arches, used as warehouses, and from above these came the almost continuous sound of trains rushing by or grinding to a halt at the station.

Today the station is all that is left of that scene. It is over fourteen years since the bulldozers moved in and demolished the rest of the area. More than that, a whole way of life was swept away at the same time which was not restored when the new blocks went up on the ruins of the old houses.

All that remained from the past were people, scattered far and wide through the Borough, and their memories. We still know many who were growing up in those days and who now have families of their own. Most of them are far better housed and have many more living facilities than they had, and one would expect them to have forgotten the old days. But no sooner do they meet us than, invariably, they exclaim with relish: 'd'you remember . . .?' With that, a reel of memories begins to whirl back, and soon a jumble of scenes and people are being re-lived, reminding me of the 'wheel of life' which a great-aunt used to operate as a treat for me when I was a small child. The black wheel, with tiny holes, would be placed on the dining table, the long strip of cartoon-like scenes would be threaded in, and I would be sat on a chair, made higher with cushions, and with elbows on the table in front of me would gaze entranced as the wheel revolved and the scenes rushed by.

My purpose in re-living some of the scenes from our

12

memory wheel of life in this account is primarily to show that in fact a continuing and powerful thread ran throughout. It brought several Christians from different backgrounds to work with us, and it brought two of us to live in the area and to share the problems common to people there. None of us arrived on the scene with any prior thought of doing this, and none of us had a conventional training for the sort of things that soon confronted us. Nor, having become involved, did we set up an organisation with specialists, to plan ahead a programme of what we should undertake, and to raise adequate finance to keep us and put the work on a secure basis. All the same, things kept happening and moving forward from one unexpected development to another. Our task, it seemed to us, was to try to be sensitive to the way we were being led and to keep up with events by thinking through, on biblical principles, how to meet and tackle the various situations in which we found ourselves. In so doing we had to learn many lessons the hard way, at first hand, about Christian life and witness in the city. And there were many lessons for us about 'the city' too.

Although this is not a sociological study, it is obviously impossible to have lived, within the space of one generation, in two distinct social structures, each a part of the 'inner city', and to have experienced their pressures, tensions and distinctive sub-cultures, without arriving at certain conclusions and challenging certain assumptions of those who look on from the outside. What for instance do we mean by 'the city'? The inner core of office land and prestigious homes? The suburban circles of a middle-class population, with tree-lined affluence increasing as the circles spread out to meet the country? Or that highly populated, densely packed ring sandwiched between the inner core and the outer suburban circles which forms the inner-city and its people? Even here two worlds co-exist: the few still remaining tightly-knit neighbourhood communities among old streets and houses such as the one we knew in the sixties, and the sprawling conglomerate of strangers inhabiting the concrete ghettoes which have largely replaced the old.

The thread which this account traces led us to live for some years in both these distinctive inner city environments, with a nightmare period of mud, noise and upheaval in between. Each period stands in sharp contrast, emphasising the traumatic upheaval in attitudes and ways of life which faced people when the bulldozers moved in to destroy their world.

Let me explain that the old houses in which families had lived, sometimes for generations, were often in poor condition, with cracks in the walls dating from the blitz, damp, without central heating and sometimes with outdoor toilets and no bathrooms. The conditions in fact were everything that we have learned to deplore, and that are constantly cited today as being major causes of social unrest. But there was another side. For all their deficiencies, the old terraced houses I remember each had their own front door, a small front garden where a few flowers could be grown, a back yard for the washing and for junk and an outside shed for bikes, a workshop and sometimes even space for hens or pigeons. No-one would breathe down your neck if it was all an untidy mess. One family I knew kept a goat for a while, but that did create trouble when it leant over the fence and ate the neighbour's washing.

In those days your house was in *your* street, and there was a sense of close-knit community. You had only to go to the front windows or the door to see someone go by and exchange a few words. Whenever you were in the house, you heard shrill familiar sounds from the street. Familiar was the word: you belonged. You knew everyone, and most of what was going on, and who came along. I remember being approached by a total stranger one day, only to find that I had been observed by her from behind net curtains for some weeks as I went up and down the road. She had made it her business to find out who I was, what I was doing, where

I came from, and so on. Another time, when I was still as I thought a stranger in the street, a child shouted after me one day: 'You've 'ad yer 'air cut'. And I had. You might row with the people next door, and have a feud with the couple opposite, but they were still part of your life, part of the identity that gave 'you' some meaning. Moreover, if you did not see them about, you would find out why, and if anything was wrong one of the neighbours would do something about it. No old person in your street lay dead for days before being found.

Then there was the corner shop, the hub of gossip and a centre of social life. There were no set opening and closing times and no impersonal uninterested staff, just Jim and Emmie, who always knew what you wanted and what day your old man got paid and when you could pay up. They were always open unless they had gone out.

There were often family ties too. Two or more generations of a family often lived in the same street, only a few doors from one another, and children grew up surrounded by relations. The street was the children's play centre, that and the dump where the houses had been bombed. A mother could let even small children out to play because they would not be far away and she could keep an eye on them from the windows or front door. If someone else's child hit hers, she could be out in a moment to thump the other back. It was that sort of close community. But there was independence too. If a man chose to paint his front door in stripes of mauve and orange, that was his affair. Or if the washing was strung across the yard, or the children brought home a puppy, these were family happenings. They were nothing to do with anyone else. A man's house might be small and damp and slummy. But it was his inviolable castle – until the bulldozers got to work and swept it all away.

Now take a look at what has replaced all that. When the tall new blocks were erected on the ruins of the houses and were ready for occupation, tenants at first moved in amid transports of delight at the gleaming well-fitted kitchens and bathrooms, the central heating and large windows. But it was not long before problems began to be felt. People opened their glossy front doors, painted the same as all the other hundreds of front doors, and looked out on to emptiness. There was either a long, bare passage punctuated by closed doors, or an empty hallway with closed doors. They were isolated from the outside world except by the lift.

Needless to say, the lift was soon out of order. In any case it only stopped at alternate floors, so that there was little chance of contact with neighbours living on the intervening floors. Inevitably it was not long before old people were afraid to go out, in case the lift was not working when they wanted to come back; or in case children, rushing along a corridor, knocked them over; or, worse, lest the shadowy ground level approaches to the lift concealed lurking muggers.

People could look out of their beautiful windows, but unless they were living on a low floor, they had little sense of social contact with the world outside. The passers by below were more like ants than humans, and the cars moved like clockwork toys. There was no familiar back yard with a comfortable wall to lean against and gossip to a neighbour; nowhere near at hand for the clutter and paraphernalia of the old shed or workshop. Washing was not allowed to be hung outside the windows. There was nowhere to grow plants, except sometimes a small balcony, nor for pigeons. Pets were not supposed to be kept at all. You were not permitted either to paint your own front door according to your fancy. In fact, there was little sense of belonging any more either to your house or to your neighbourhood.

For people with young children there was worse to contend with. Either the mother had to keep her children cooped up in the flat, or, if they went down in the lift alone, they were out of sight and removed from any contact with the parent. They were not in 'our street' any more, but in a large, alien world, where the

16

mother had no means of knowing what trouble they might get into, nor who was bullying or even attacking them. Sometimes they came home without their toys; their bikes had been stolen; their jerseys were either lost or taken away from them. While this was a nightmare for many mothers, wondering what was going on, the alternative – having them cooped up all day in the living room – was little better. Is it any wonder that young mums, and not so young, have been going to the doctor for tranquillisers? Or that the new blocks have proved to be a breeding ground for neurosis?

For the adolescent there was little outlet for his energies. Who at that age wants an organised playground? Even if it is an 'Adventure playground' – it is still planned; it is still stamped, *The Authorities say 'play here'*. So boredom sets in, punctuated by sporadic drives of uncoordinated energy that find an outlet in smashing, fighting and thieving, although that is not true for all of course. The natural conformists and the children of a closely knit, disciplined home would not go out on the rampage in the evenings. They have homework and leisure interests, and take part in organised group activities at various youth clubs. But these are a small minority. A depressing number of other children are, however, growing up in fear of mixing with their contemporaries, living isolated in their concrete boxes. And there is yet another category: those who are regularly locked in by parents who go out to work or to drink in the evenings. To communicate with these you have to talk through the letter boxes to watchful eyes. And sometimes as you walk the concrete wastes below and look up, you will see silent, staring little figures looking down on you from the heights.

The serious social effects of living in these high-rise blocks of concrete are only too well recognised now. But it is depressing that at the time when so many of the new estates were still being dreamed up by men with drawing boards and no dimensions apart from economic ones,

17

apparently Christian architects as well as Christians in local and national government failed to think these concepts through seriously and clearly in the light of Christian principles or to speak out positively about the dangerously dehumanising factors inherent in those attractive drawings. For the tragic fact is that, in spite of armies of social and community workers who have been busy, and the multiplicity of reports that have appeared, and schemes that have been sponsored, the teething problems of life on the new estates were as nothing to what has developed since. Loneliness, discontent, depression, frustration and violence all abound. And *fear*. Acres of underground garages stand empty as a result of continual thefts and vandalism. People approach the imposing pillared entrances to tower blocks warily even in daylight, because those pillars that looked so nice on the drawings seem perfectly designed for muggers. The main doorways, once unenclosed, now have heavy locked doors, and an intercom system has been put in to all flats for the safety of tenants. Even as I write, one of the new estates which I watched being built on the ruins of the old houses is being systematically and totally evacuated.

This present account stops short at the great upheaval which transformed a neighbourhood community of old-established ways into a wasteland of concrete. But the thread of events which concerns us and which began in the old environment was to lead straight on in unbroken line into the as yet uncharted and formidable currents of life on the estates. Without the earlier crucial years of this account, however, there would have been no continuing thread for us. We would have had no place in the new scene; no preparation or close ties with a host of bewildered people; and no experience of their problems. More important, we should not ourselves have experienced in the same degree the incredible, but true, faithfulness of God. In fact, without those early years there would be no story to tell.

1: Not in Word Only

The 49 passes the opulent Royal Garden Hotel, and if you are sitting on the near side you may gaze out across Kensington Gardens to the mellow rose-red Palace, before the bus makes a sharp righthand turn and stops at the top of Palace Gate. That is where I got on it the first time I went to Clapham Junction in search of a disused chapel which I had been told about. At the time I was sharing a basement flat in one of the pleasant quiet roads leading up to Kensington Gardens. I had not lived there very long, but the neighbourhood had old associations for me. My grandparents had lived near by and I was born in their house. Until I was about six years old my parents and I had lived not far away and I had recollections of Sunday walks in the Gardens, up the Broad Walk to the Round Pond or sometimes, less interesting to me, along the Flower Walk where the grown-ups enthused and our Cairn terrier and I drooped and lagged behind. In those days the great elm trees still lined the Broad Walk and children with uniformed nannies played round the pond. I had a dim memory too of an old lady sitting at the gate with bunches of balloons for sale.

The bus ride from Palace Gate to Clapham Junction threaded its way through Kensington and Chelsea, and then branched south across the river into an unfamiliar world. This was Battersea. Stark warehouses lined the river frontage, with barges moored alongside. On one side a grimy factory disgorged smoke. The bus route lay through streets of small shops and pubs and skirted one end of a crowded street market, before I saw a railway bridge ahead and a major cross roads, flanked by a large department store. I had arrived at the Junction.

I had been directed to the house of the chapel caretaker. This proved to be an old lady who had taken care of the place since an even older lady, Miss Potter, had died aged over ninety. As I was to discover, most people round about had known and respected Miss Potter, who had spent years of faithful loving care in trying to keep the chapel open, with an ever shrinking congregation as the neighbourhood changed, until only she and the present caretaker and one other elderly woman remained. From then on the inside of the chapel was cleaned and cared for, but it stood empty.

The caretaker and I walked round to see the place. It stood plain and sturdy on a street corner, with some of its high windows broken by children playing outside. We entered at the side, into what was called the School Hall, a severe, high-roofed room with built in cupboards along one side, holding a number of old hymn books and Bibles. Along the other wall were rows of hooks, where victorian children must have hung their coats neatly before sitting down on the rows of wooden benches. All the woodwork was painted a dark chocolate colour. Two small rooms led off this hall. One had obviously been a vestry, and had a bookshelf and an antiquated gas fire. This I mentally reserved for my office. The other room had a door leading out to the back yard where there were two toilets, and a doorway with steps down to the cellar. This last extended under both back rooms and housed an ancient boiler, only part of which could be seen as the cellar was submerged under several feet of water. Not until we tried to pump this out later did we realise that the course of an underground river flowed through it. I had never before seen so many rats.

Large doors led from the schoolroom to the main chapel where generations of devout chapel-goers had met Sunday by Sunday to worship God. It remained an interesting period piece with a circular central pulpit on which lay the open Bible, emphasising the centrality of the Word and of preaching from it, and in front of it the platform where the Communion table had once stood. Beneath that, though unknown to me at that time, lay the baptistry. This only came to light by chance when a lad turned on an interesting tap half hidden beside the platform. Hours later a pool of water spread across the floor, and on prising up the platform we found an overflowing tiled pool below. There was an organ at the back and an overhead gallery suspended on pillars. Four heavy wrought iron lights hung from the high roof. Their strength was put to the test one night when Bill, one of the lads we grew to know well, wild and redheaded, leapt with a Tarzan call from the gallery to swing on those lights, without damage to them or himself.

The reason I had come to this chapel was that I was looking for somewhere to house the *Evangelical Magazine* which a group of us had begun to publish several months before. The main aims were to be both pastoral, and to think through every-day problems, trying to show the relevance of the Christian faith in every sphere of life. I had become the managing editor of our magazine, although highly unsuited to the job, since I was no sort of practical businesswoman. The two consulting editors lived far away: Jim Parker, an Anglican theologian, was then in Bristol and later in Oxford, and Elwyn Davies, the General Secretary of the Evangelical Movement of Wales, was firmly entrenched in Wales and Welsh affairs. A third consultant was Raymond Johnston, Lecturer in Education at a Northern university, who has since become more widely known for his outspoken stand on a number of moral issues, in his capacity as General Secretary of the Festival of Light (now known as Care Trust). We had launched the magazine with zeal but without financial backing, and whilst its circulation was growing and covering our printing costs, there was nothing left over to rent any premises. To begin with, my room at the flat was our combined office and store, but soon there would be no room for me! It was at this seeming *impasse* that I heard about the empty chapel which belonged to the Association of Strict Baptists. Having seen the place, I knew that it would be damp; but it provided plenty of room and, most important, it was offered for our use rent-free. Surely, this was Providence; and gratefully we accepted.

The chapel had electric light, but its only heating was the submerged boiler. As we took the place over in the late summer this did not trouble us to begin with. Bob moved our magazine stock and such office equipment as we had, in his van after work. It took several journeys from Kensington to the Junction, and all of us who were concerned with the magazine met at the chapel to store things away. Everyone was a 'voluntary helper', giving their time after whatever regular job they had. Bob was in insurance, and after long, exacting office hours did an incredible amount for the magazine, organising its despatch and looking after the accounts. Most of those first helpers belonged, as he and I both did, to Westminster Chapel. Among them I first met Rosemary, a physiotherapist, and her two friends, Jill, then also a physiotherapist, and Stacey, who taught at Putney High School. My reason for singling them out in particular is that for twenty years Rosemary has been totally involved with the work that has developed, and her two friends still take an active interest. In those early days they lived in Putney, but other helpers had more awkward journeys to make to reach the Junction. They had to venture along unfamiliar, ill-lit side-roads, with uneven pavements and occasional dark passage-ways where groups of youngsters huddled, shadowy and vaguely menacing. Looking back at those times, the devotion of those helpers to the magazine was quite amazing.

Since Westminster Chapel, or rather, its very remarkable ministry in those days, was not only the spiritual home of most of those who helped, but was also to have close ties with everything that happened later, I need to relate how this came about. In particular, as this necessarily implies the record of my own involvement, I should explain how I, who grew up outside any church circle or christian commitment, and had often scorned those who seemed to me glibly to conform to tradition and conventional 'nice' behaviour, came to take on a disused chapel in order to house the *Evangelical Magazine*.

At that time, under the influence of Dr Lloyd-Jones, Westminster Chapel was surely the most cosmopolitan and truly ecumenical church in London. It drew people of all sorts. Many professional men and women attended, as did large numbers of students from the University and from medical schools. There were people of all ages, and though by its situation in the heart of office-land, it was not a 'local' church, numbers of young families travelled considerable distances to spend Sundays there. An appreciable sprinkling of manual workers came, and even one or two members of the aristocracy. This conglomerate was made up from many denominations – Anglicans, Brethren, Roman Catholics, Methodists, Presbyterians, Congregationalists, Salvationists, Pentecostals and others who, like me, had come in from outside any Christian connection. They were not all British, nor white. I remember a contingent of Chinese used to sit up in the gallery every week; Africans and West-Indians were dotted about the congregation. I met an Arab member of the church and several Jews. There were South-Africans, Americans, and people from most European countries on both sides of the Iron Curtain.

I knew none of this, however, when I first walked into the chapel. I was spending a weekend in the house of Dr Margery Blackie, who was later to become Physician to the Queen. My mother had known her for years, and had first taken me to her as a patient when I was four years old. Just before the war ended, I had arrived home from India on my own, very unwell with chronic intestinal troubles and had gone at once to Dr Blackie. She had not only treated me over the next years but had shown me much kindness, and I had come to know the household in South Kensington very well. I doubt if anyone else would have got me to go to a church and a nonconformist chapel at that. I do not think that I had ever been to a chapel before, and I remember looking round somewhat furtively as we walked up the entrance steps, to make sure that no one I knew was passing by.

On entering I found myself in an oval vaulted building, with two tiers of galleries. The far end was dominated by a circular pulpit of dark mahogany, behind which reared the organ. But I had little time to get my bearings. Dr Blackie, always a brisk walker, was half way down an aisle. I followed, and we sat down in a pew almost at the front. We were soon joined by an elderly, somewhat severe looking woman to whom I was introduced in undertones – Miss Mildred Cable. The name was familiar. I had read her remarkable account of travels in the Gobi Desert, and I was impressed to find her in the chapel.

The service began when a slight figure in a severe black Geneva gown ascended the pulpit and took his stand behind a huge open Bible. I had no idea who he was, and in any case the name of Dr Lloyd-Jones would have meant nothing to me. But I soon became aware that the service was very different from any I had hitherto sat through during my occasional visits to the village church, usually at Christmas and Easter, when I was at home with my parents. There was no choir, but the singing was hearty. Several hundred people made up the congregation and, as I glanced about me, I was struck by the fact that most of them were obviously paying close attention, even opening Bibles to follow the readings for themselves instead of drowsily thinking their own thoughts.

But it was the sermon itself that arrested me. This was no brief homily delivered in the detached rather colourless manner which I associated with sermons. The preacher began by laying down certain propositions, which were provocative to my way of thinking, and then reasoning and arguing them through. This was stimulating and I soon began mentally to pick holes in his arguments, only to find that a few minutes later he would raise my very objections and answer them. But I was roused, and continued to listen critically. The sermon itself was based on the story of the Prodigal Son, that I do remember. But the points that caught my attention at the time have long been forgotten. In fact, they soon left my mind. What most deeply impressed me was not only that this man was prepared to encourage his congregation to think – his sermon was no 'opium for the people' – but also that it was no academic discourse given by someone detached from his subject. The man spoke with a passionate conviction and depth of concern which I could not doubt: he really did believe what he said! Moreover he spoke with a directness that was new to me, almost as if he was addressing me personally and challenging my assumptions. When we emerged from the chapel my thoughts were in some turmoil, and I was amazed to find that the service had lasted for an hour and a half.

That evening still had another memorable experience in store. Dr Blackie had arranged to drive Miss Cable home, and since I was with her I went too. On the way Dr Blackie said that she must drop in on an old patient. When we arrived outside the house she went in but soon came back to say that her patient would like to meet Miss Cable. Again, since I was with them, I was asked in too and found myself being introduced to Dame Myra Hess. I sat and looked round while the others talked and I still have a picture of the scene in my mind. We were in a peaceful sitting room with long windows through which the evening sun shone, burnishing a bowl of roses which stood on a low table by the window. Presently Dame Myra went to the piano, and as the gold light slowly faded the limpid notes of 'Jesu, Joy of Man's Desiring' and 'Sheep May Safely Graze' filled the room.

In spite of the impression that evening made, I did not return to Westminster Chapel when, soon afterwards, I came to live in London. It was to be several years before apparently unrelated events brought me back. By then I was writing minor scripts for the BBC, mostly for musical biographies, and adapting musical comedies. One day I received a letter asking if I would prepare a programme on the history of the Bible's transmission. This was completely unknown territory to me. I did not read the Bible and had never thought about, or learnt, how it has survived the centuries. Nor was I particularly interested. The same day that I wrote to refuse the offer, I met an old friend at the BBC and jokingly told him about the proposal. To my surprise he took it seriously and argued that it would be good experience for me to branch out into a new field. In the end he not only persuaded me to accept the chance but managed to retrieve my original letter.

Very soon I began to have strong misgivings. I had to start my researches somewhere, and since I was a reader at what was then the British Museum Reading Room, I went there. But the great circular stands of catalogues contained literally thousands of entries for books dealing with some part of the Bible's transmission. I was appalled and to begin with, chose books at random. This was a recipe for hopeless confusion. However, slowly, the majestic sweep of events down the centuries began to emerge, and into this chronology I was able to slot outstanding incidents and people. Since I had always been interested in history, I began to find it a fascinating study.

As I went on, two underlying themes gripped me, and began to mould the shape of my prospective script. The first was the immensity of the background tapestry into which the story of the Bible's transmission was inter-woven. Seemingly unrelated world events, and the rise and fall of empires and nations, somehow worked in together to further the Bible's dissemination. I remember how I was struck by facts of the state of the Roman Empire just at the time when the first Christian missionaries set out to travel Europe with the 'Good News', and were followed by letters and copies of the gospels, and then of the whole Bible. For that was the very time when travel was made possible throughout the Empire which sprawled across Europe, with its arteries of great roads, its common language of culture — Greek — and the dispersion of Roman troops and comparative safety of travel.

Then I was confronted with the fact that when the New Testament had come into existence, and there was need to spread the Bible, this coincided with vellum, that tough leather material, beginning to replace the earlier fragile papyrus for making books. Then again I was confronted by the fact of the fall of Constantinople to the Turks a thousand years later in 1453, which led to priceless Greek Bible manuscripts, unknown in Western Europe for a thousand years, being brought into the West by refugee Greek scholars only to be followed the very next year, 1454, by the invention of printing. So, when the great impetus for Bible translation sprang from the Reformation, there were Greek texts available to compare with the Latin, and there was printing to spread thousands of Bibles in the time it had previously taken laboriously to write out one manuscript. These were but a few of the more dramatic events that I saw weaving and interweaving to bring about my story.

The other aspect which impressed me was the moving pageant of people all down the centuries who had been involved in carrying on and handing down the Bible. I found myself confronted by a long, unbroken line of men, women and children, some famous, others obscure, who had evidently found the Bible so precious that they had gladly risked their lives to safeguard it and to hand it down to future generations. I do not think that I had ever heard of William Tyndale before, and had had no idea of how this remarkable Book had been translated into English. Nor had I heard of the Lollards and their sufferings with Wyclif over the translation of the Book, nor of the ordinary people, shepherds, peasants and townsfolk, who had given almost all they possessed in order to buy portions of the Book in

English. As I read, this pageant of people seemed to be crying out to me: 'We died to hand the book down. Can't you even be bothered to read it? Does your freedom to read when you like mean so little?'

In the course of my reading, I came across a brief book by Mildred Cable about what the Bible had meant to various people down the centuries. I therefore wrote to her, reminding her of our meeting, and asking if I might bring my draft material and go over it with her. I received an invitation to tea, and in due course arrived at the Hampstead flat which Miss Cable shared with the two companions of her Mongolian travels, Francesca and Evangeline French, and with Topsy, the deaf and dumb Mongolian girl who had been for sale for a few shillings in a remote Mongolian market. She had lived with Miss Cable and the others ever since, and was now no longer even a young woman.

Miss Cable was helpful over my material and I was interested in her comments. When I got up to go, Miss Cable said: 'You've talked a lot about the Bible's history. What do you *believe* about the Book?' This silenced me. 'I don't know,' I said at last. 'Well, isn't it time you found out?' she replied. It was spoken in a cold matter-of-fact tone that stung me, as no doubt it was intended to. For I took a pride in an intelligent reasoned approach to what I believed and did. But was I being intelligent to become deeply impressed by the facts of the Bible's transmission, and still not to read the Book or to make up my mind about the contents?

That evening I began to read the New Testament, starting with the four gospels. I was living in a rambling house just off Oxford Street, where I had a room on the first floor with a small balcony opening off it, from which I could just see the throngs of people. It was the end of June, and very hot, and when I had the window open the noise of traffic formed the background to my reading. I had not gone far before I found my previous assumptions to be hopelessly inadequate. I had always dismissed the teachings of Jesus Christ as great, though impossible, ideals, but, as I now realised, I had never studied what in fact he had said. Now, what I was confronted with on every page was not so much a set of ethical teachings, as the person of Christ himself. It was he who dominated what I read; everything pointed to him; he was the person who gave meaning to the extraordinary statements that stared at me. Just a great idealist, a reformer, who had lived before his time? But that was not the person who was presented here. That person made staggering claims for himself, as *being* the Way to God, not as teaching us the way; as having *in himself* the *power* to bring people to God and to give them eternal life, not just to talk about the way; as being *himself* the Truth; . . . as being alive here and now! *'Come to me'*, he kept saying, *'Trust me'* . . . *'Believe in ME'* . . . *'You shall know ME'* . . . and so on. The further I went, the more clearly an issue stood out: either the man had been a madman, or else he was who and what he said he was – the Son of God.

But was it really so hard to decide? Could anybody who had produced such supremely wise and uplifting teaching, possibly have been mad? But if not, and if he was who he said he was, then I was facing a new dimension. If he *is* – then he is *now*. That was the revolutionary and staggering view that opened up to me. For if he is *now*, then obviously all of life, and the world itself, has to be seen within an eternal dimension in which he cannot be ignored or evaded. Over and over again, I found myself thinking: If he is, then he *is*. He is *here and now*. Why on earth had I never thought of this before? Why had I assumed that Christianity was simply a moral code? Why hadn't I thought it important to find out more about it? For what I was reading was the most revolutionary concept I had ever been confronted with. It meant viewing one's whole life within a new dimension, and this clearly changed the meaning of everything. Moreover, it held out the most amazing offers and promises: a purpose and fulfilment in life now, and an exciting future. Present peace, joy, security, understanding, all the things people were always looking for.

It was the time of the Summer Sales in Oxford Street. All day long crowds of bargain-hunters jostled and pushed one another in their efforts to secure a bargain. Whenever I went out, I had to struggle through those crowds, and all the time it seemed to me that towering over us and that seedy street, was the figure of that Person. I felt like shouting out: 'There's something much greater on offer. Why aren't you even bothering to find out what Jesus Christ says? Why ignore his extraordinary claims and promises? Why not find out what you believe, and if you can't believe in the end, why aren't you sad about it?' But of course, I was really shouting to myself. I had been no different from most of those bargain-hunters. Christ and his claims had never seemed to me to enter into real life at all.

The next Sunday I went to Westminster Chapel again. The place was much as I remembered it; the congregation was perhaps even larger, but the same preacher was in the pulpit. This time he read from Isaiah chapter 55, and took the first two verses as the subject of his sermon:

'Ho! Everyone who thirsts, Come to the waters;
And you who have no money, Come, buy and eat.
Yes, come, buy wine and milk Without money and
without price.
Why do you spend money for what is not bread,
And your wages for what does not satisfy?
Listen diligently to me, and hear what is good,
And let your soul delight itself in abundance.'

Why, asked that uncomfortably penetrating preacher, did people spend their time going after things that would not last, instead of seeking the only way to a satisfaction, fulfilment and happiness that would not pass away? Again, he laid down his proposition and argued his case. This time I did not mentally argue back,

30

since he was uttering the very thoughts that had been causing me turmoil all the week. Instead I thought with relief that the revolutionary concept of an entirely new dimension in which to view the whole of life that had so shattered me was not a symptom of madness in me after all! Here was this undoubtedly sane, intelligent man, saying the same thing and pointing to the same person, as being alive and holding life and truth in his hands. The issue as I had seen it was a real one.

When the service ended, I did not go and speak to that preacher. Instead I went home and did not return to the Chapel for nearly six months. I am well aware now of a popular notion among many concerned Christians, that people need to be pressurised into some commitment to Christ when they begin to show any interest, and that they must not be allowed to go off on their own in case they lose interest. I cannot accept that view, since if the Holy Spirit of God is not more powerful than our efforts in leading people to God, then we have no gospel worth having. For such a view would make people more powerful than God. In my own case, the Holy Spirit was to prove a lot more powerful than my objections and attempts to put the gospels and their story out of my mind.

Although I had been intellectually persuaded of the reality of the issue with which Jesus Christ confronted me, I soon realised that this, if worked out, would involve more than intellectual acceptance. It would obviously mean that I must change my way of life, which clearly did not fit in with what Christ had to say. Moreover, it would mean actually giving up things which I enjoyed for the sake of someone whom I must believe though I did not see or know him. That was the rub. Could I do that? As weeks and months went by, the tensions mounted. At times I decided to forget the whole thing and go on as I had been before. But I found that I could not forget. That elusive, but dominating figure would not be forgotten. So I would veer to the opposite tack, and decide that I must put everything else aside and try to discover more about him. But inevitably, as soon as I did that, something cropped up to lure me back to the old ways which could not happily co-exist with thoughts of him. So it went on, and far from being full of joy and peace and understanding, I began to think that I had never been more miserable and that a life-time committed to struggling along in a sort of blind belief in someone, somewhere, would be intolerable. I could never manage that. On the other hand, I could not go on, with thoughts of him coming into my mind and refusing to disappear.

At last, I could go on no longer. Whatever it meant, however hopeless it would be to try to trust him, I could do nothing but submit myself to this unknown person whom I did not know but whose claims I could not go on ignoring even if it meant nothing but struggles and doubts. It was far from being a thankful or grateful submission but rather a grudging surrender, which makes what happened then the more amazing. For if we do not think much of people who give us a grudging acceptance, how much more might he rightfully refuse to meet with such a person? But he did not. Surrendering into what I thought was the unknown, I found myself flooded by knowledge, surrounded by a realised presence more real than furniture and room around me. He was with me. I had not got to go on struggling alone after all. *'I am with you'* . . . *'I will never leave you'* . . . *'I will dwell with you'* – his words rang in my head.

But, of course, in time a reaction set in. Again and more strongly, the thought returned: *I must be going mad.* This could not happen. I must have imagined it. I remember coming home a day or two later on top of a bus, and every lurch and stop seemed to echo: *mad – mad – you are mad.* But I could still work, and carry on living and go shopping. Surely I could not be completely insane!

In this turbulence, I returned to Westminster Chapel. Again, there was the same large company; the same austere black figure in the pulpit. This time he directed us to Paul's first letter to the Thessalonians, chapter 1, verse 5. I had no idea where to find this in the Bible supplied in the pew where I sat, so I listened to the words:

> 'For our Gospel did not come to you in word only, but also in power, and in the Holy Spirit, and in much assurance.'

There could hardly have been a more complete answer to my dilemma. These words, as they were expounded, were an exact analysis of what happened to me. The relief! I was not mad. The person of Christ was real. What was more, and however unbelievable, it was true that he knew me and had made himself known to me.

When the service was over, my relief and sense of deliverance was so great that I went round to see the preacher. Much to my surprise, the authoritative austere person of the pulpit proved to be the kindliest, most approachable of men. Even more helpful to me who had never spoken to a minister on spiritual matters in my life, he was extraordinarily easy to speak to. I told him of my previous visits to the Chapel, and he remarked calmly, 'So I *was* speaking to you. I knew those sermons were for *someone* in the congregation.'

After that I began going to the Chapel regularly. I soon met people there, and as old cronies tended to drift away when they knew I 'had seen the light', at the same time I was getting to know new friends and discovering that all of them had in different ways been led into a knowledge of Christ himself. Far from being out on a limb, I was in good company. But I did not conform too easily to many church-going habits and my old rebellious instincts and critical attitudes did not drop away. Why the evangelical jargon? And why so much of a middle-class sub-culture? But two people who certainly had none of these and who wisely and unobtrusively guided me away from an initial sinking feeling, that somehow or another I would have to try to conform to a pattern, were Dr and Mrs Lloyd-Jones. Their patience and readiness to listen to my arguments and reactions was extraordinary, and looking back to those days, I see clearly how much they both helped to prepare me for what was coming – my plunge into the totally different sub-culture of Battersea in the sixties.

2. Mount Sinai Comes to Clapham Junction

When we moved the *Evangelical Magazine* to the old chapel near the Junction, we had no particular interest in the neighbourhood. I think that to begin with we all regarded the streets round the chapel simply as rather insalubrious ways of reaching our destination. No more. Nor did it occur to us that we might be arousing curiosity. But it was not long before children's faces peered in through the windows, and eyes looked through the keyhole of the main door. Sometimes there were scuffles outside and a ball would come flying through the top of a broken window. When we left the building at night, a few youngsters would be watching from a distance.

I soon began to have uncomfortable thoughts. Here we were, publishing and despatching the *Evangelical Magazine*, which was concerned to apply and present our faith with relevance to our present world and day to day living in it. Yet, we were apparently blind to a mission field on our doorstep. What about these children who had been busy breaking the chapel windows for months? They obviously had no church connections. If our faith was real to us, should we not open a Sunday-school in the chapel for them? But, if so, who should run it? It was not my scene, and I did not think that our various magazine helpers could undertake any more. How wrong I was! Yet at the time it seemed that way, and I took the problem to the wise and patient minister of Westminster Chapel, Dr Lloyd-Jones. He was sympathetic and, as always, constructive. He suggested that the London City Mission might help.

Their missioners assisted various Christian organisations and churches to run Sunday meetings. They might be able to help us.

On enquiry we found that the City Mission already had a missioner in the neighbourhood of the chapel, who visited from door to door, and he would welcome the opportunity of running a Sunday-school in the building. I therefore thankfully left the entire project to the care of Mr and Mrs Denton who, in due course, opened a Sunday afternoon meeting for children of the families they visited. The Dentons had worked in the area for several years and had no illusions about the hardness of their task and the apparent unresponsiveness of most of the population. So they were not deterred by the mere handful of small children who came on Sundays.

By this time I was on speaking terms with various groups of children whom I passed on my way along the road: 'Why not pop over to the chapel on Sundays?' I used to ask. But I was met with derisory giggles or flat refusals.

Sometimes I looked in on Sunday afternoons, when about half a dozen tidily dressed and nicely behaved little children sat on a bench learning to sing choruses, listening to Bible stories illustrated by flannelgraphs, and then colouring texts and pictures to take home with them. One afternoon from that initial period stands out in my memory. It was the occasion of the first Children's Christmas Party. I had been invited to drop in, and drove down with a friend. It was cold and dark and the usual yellow murkiness hung over the streets, a combination of bad street lighting and the evening mistiness hanging very low above the ground. The chapel outline was gaunt, but lights shone welcomingly from the hall. We opened the door and stepped in. The Dentons and their helpers had worked hard: the chocolate-brown walls were gay with streamers and paper chains. Immediately below the central hanging lights stood a long trestle table covered in a white sheet.

On it were piled home-made cakes and sandwiches, biscuits, jellies, mugs of orange-juice and crackers, and round it sat ten little children in their best clothes, hair shining, mouths busy, hands reaching out. All the light and life and colour in the stark hall were caught in that central pool of light. Beyond it the hall faded in shadows. But here, at its centre, it seemed to me was a pledge of new life arising after long declining years since the chapel had known spiritual life and activity. The scene moved me, but it also made me uneasy. What I saw had the flavour of a Dickens-style Christmas card. What had this to do with the hordes of shrill-voiced, grimy youngsters of today who played in the streets outside? Obviously, in their minds, nothing – or some of them would have been inside.

The Sunday-school, however, was not the project which most concerned me in the neighbourhood for the time being. In my talks with the old lady who had looked after the chapel I had heard about the Women's Meeting which Miss Potter had run for many years, and how the last few survivors had missed it when it had to close. I wondered whether, since we were using their old chapel, we should try to re-open the meeting. Possibly I would have stopped at the mere thought of it, had I not met Mrs Cherry, whose husband was the General Secretary of the Ceylon and India General Mission. Although she and her husband now lived in London, she was still a missionary at heart and warmed to the idea of working among women in our area. She agreed to spend one or two afternoons every week in house to house visiting with a view to encouraging folk to come to a meeting. I felt that I could do no less, although I had never visited anyone from door to door before. We obtained various little booklets and wrote out notices about the Sunday-school and the proposed Women's Meeting, and armed with these we set out, taking a road each.

I wish now that I had kept some record of those afternoons. What I most remember is not what I achieved in talking to the people, but the impact which they made on me and the amount that I learnt from them.

Even in the small neighbourhood which we visited, there were social distinctions between the various roads, and sometimes between sides of the same road. For instance one side of a nearby road had delightful early Victorian cottages, where roses and clematis and hollyhocks bloomed. Had these been in Chelsea or Kensington they would have been worth a small fortune. But as yet Battersea was largely 'undiscovered', and now these buildings have all been bulldozed into oblivion. Many of the inhabitants were elderly, and had inherited their cottages from parents, or had lived all their married lives in them. Some had divided their house and a younger generation of the family shared it. Nearer to the main road, these cottages gave way to high terraced houses where the steps always seemed to be swarming with children.

On the opposite side of that road I remember two households in particular. One might have belonged to relations of Steptoe & Son – the father and son were 'totters' (rag and bone men) and had a horse and cart. Where they kept the horse I do not know, but the contents of the cart were kept in the house and littered the yard. The other family I came to know very well had three sons at school and father did a variety of jobs, including being a dustman for a while. We shared a liking for pickled onions and every autumn he would acquire a sack of onions. His house would then steam and reek for days, after which he would send me over a large old-fashioned sweet jar full of pickled onions. One day he drove up to the chapel door with a van from which he unloaded a present of a bedroom suite and a pianola, complete with dozens of rolls of old-time music.

On another occasion I had a memorable drive across London with him in his van, which had recently been carrying loads of manure. Mercifully it was a bitter winter's morning or the smell would have been overpowering. On the way he told me that there had been a thick fog at six o'clock that morning when he had arrived at the crematorium to do a bit of work on the ovens. Most improbably, we were on our way to the Arsenal Football Ground to meet a man I was in contact with who ran a farm for rehabilitating drug addicts. It was an excellent work and I was hopeful that my friend's eldest son, who was taking heroin, would be able to go there.

Mrs Cherry and I had chosen to go visiting in the afternoons. I soon found out that this was not a good time; on the other hand, it was hard to find a more suitable one in the crowded life which most of the women led. Many formed part of the 'army' of Mrs Mops who set out at six am. to clean offices in Whitehall, Victoria and the City. Others went off a bit later to 'do' for wealthy employers in Chelsea. They would shop on their way home before starting on their own cleaning and washing and preparing an evening meal for when their children and menfolk came in. It is remarkable that, being disturbed in the middle of their afternoon, most were polite and patient when they answered my knock. Only very occasionally was the door shut in my face. Usually, when it had been established that I was not from the insurance, nor was I selling anything, I was listened to as a I tried to explain why I believed it important for them, and their children, to make time to consider what God has told us about ourselves and the world and how to cope with our lives. They would nod, many would agree and would take a leaflet and say they would remember to come to the Women's Meeting. Some however invariably commented, 'Yes, well I'm not really religious though I always say my prayers. But I haven't time to go to meetings.' And that was that.

Years later, when I was regarded as part of the scene, I understood their reactions. Sometimes an evangelistic campaign would be organised by missions or churches from far away, and for a week or two people would spend all day visiting the houses. Often they would go away claiming to have had a wonderful response from the people to whom they talked. What they did not understand was the patient politeness of those, summoned from cooking or washing or from a hard-earned few minutes with their feet up, who agreed to everything in the hope of soon getting rid of the visitor and hurrying back to the *realities* of the day. To them, the visitors – and that meant us too in the early days – might just as well have come from Mars. They were strangers to real life in that neighbourhood. What did they know about its problems and worries, and how would they cope if faced with some of the difficulties?

There were of course exceptions among those I visited. There were elderly people who lived alone and welcomed company. They asked me inside and gave me cups of tea. Some had been brought up to go to Sunday-school and chapel. They had some knowledge of the Bible and were ready to talk about 'the good old days' when family life had meant more and children had been brought up strictly, not like the terrible goings on today! One very elderly woman was anxious for me to come back and meet her recently widowered son. I think that she wanted to get him respectably settled again!

The young women were usually on the point of rushing out to collect children from school. They listened with half an ear, then said that they believed that five-year-old Tommy or six-year-old Tracey should make up their own minds. They would tell them about Sundays, and leave it to them – Sorry, but they must dash – Bye, bye.

Those visits certainly had the effect of taking me back to the Bible and its principles. More clearly than ever before I became convinced of the importance of Christians living among people and sharing the everyday life of others, so that they could be known and seen to face the same problems as those to whom they spoke. After all, wasn't Christ himself the supreme example? He left heaven and actually lived among us, not issuing edicts from some protected ivory palace, but sharing in the troubles, the work, and the whole life of everyday people. Then there were also the first Christian missionaries. Paul, maybe the greatest of them all, did not pay hurried visits. He would remain in one place, teaching and speaking and being seen, for months, sometimes years. When he moved on, he would leave behind a little community of Christians who would go on living there and witnessing by their lives as well as by what they said. Yet it seemed that by and large today committed Christians were missing from areas like this one I was getting to know. What had happened?

Mrs Cherry with a great deal more missionary experience than I, had more successful spiritual talks with many she visited and high hopes when the time came for the first women's meeting. In the event these were dashed. A handful only turned up, almost all of whom were very elderly and had known the chapel and 'Miss Potter' long ago.

Looking back, what stands out most clearly are the mistakes I made in those first meetings. It is amazing that anyone continued to come at all. For one thing, I had decided to hold meetings in the evenings. This meant that old ladies had to go out in the cold, and trudge along ill-lit, uneven pavements to get there. As if that was not deterrent enough, the hall was chilly and the only seating was on backless benches.

Then there were the meetings themselves. We, that is, the helpers, were all as I now see, reacting against a type of superficial women's meeting, consisting solely of choruses, tea and gossip, and a sentimental chat. Instead, we went to the other extreme. Seated uncomfortably on their forms, the old ladies listened (or slumbered) through solid exegesis of Scripture passages that, with hindsight, I am sure went on too long and attempted too much. We did struggle through a hymn or two, and finish with tea and biscuits, but the meeting as a whole was an indigestible diet. Slowly however, we did learn, and though several of the women left off coming, others arrived, and during the next years we were to know some beautiful characters whose faith shone in all the very real trials of their lives and who, with very little in the way of material goods of their own, never tired of helping one another. They did us a world of good, and I still miss the fellowship of these women's meetings.

To begin with, however, it looked as if our efforts were simply going to result in perpetuating the old ways of a small in-group of women who wanted things to remain as they always had been, and establishing a Sunday-school with a tiny group of children who were unrepresentative of the mass of the people living round about. And no doubt this is all that would have happened had not events occurred to shake us out of those patterns.

The first of these was that the City Missioner was moved to another district. After a number of barren years round the Junction, the Mission had decided to withdraw from such a stony ground. This left us with the problem of who was to run the Sunday-school. Once again we turned to Westminster Chapel, and after thought and discussion a member of the Chapel volunteered. He had been involved in various Sunday-schools in suburban areas and was used to quietly mannered children and to the long-established patterns of such meetings. He therefore stepped into the breach easily with our few children, and to begin with the pattern continued unchanged.

The next event, however, disrupted that. It happened in the course of one of the Women's Meetings. It was early spring by then, and chilly in the evenings. The few women sat huddled at the end of the forms nearest to an oil stove which disgorged fumes and a little heat. That evening we had a guest speaker, Mr Micklewright, a deacon of Westminster Chapel. He had chosen as his text *One there is that sticketh closer than a brother*, and his discourse was designed primarily to encourage the sixty- to eighty-year-old age group. Suddenly, the street door burst open, there were giggles and scuffles, a ball bounced on the floor, and someone protesting loudly was shoved in to collect it while grinning faces framed the door. Obviously I had not been paying close attention to the discourse, for I moved quicker than the small boy and was at the door before he was able to recapture the ball and make his escape.

'Come on in everyone,' I invited.

This response was evidently so unexpected that it paralysed the boys. They shuffled in embarrassed, and I sat down with them, the ball in my hands, on the form at the back. 'We're having a meeting,' I explained, and you are quite welcome.'

Valiantly Mr Micklewright contined, now with two distinct audiences. I could not see the disapproval on the faces of the ladies, but I did note their rigid backs and the occasional fierce glares they directed in our direction at some particularly loud scuffle. As for the back row, I sat between the group of some six boys aged between ten and fourteen. They were fortunately still numb from the shock of finding themselves in a Ladies' Bible Meeting, and apart from nudges, a few giggles, and scuffling of feet, we sat in an uneasy row – with me probably more uneasy than any now that I realised how impossible a captive audience I had foisted on the speaker. Somehow Mr Micklewright continued and brought the meeting to a thankful close. The boys and I moved smartly to the door, where I gave them their ball and invited them warmly to the afternoon Sunday-school. We then parted with them grinning and escaping fast. I returned to face the ladies' disapproval.

I had little thought of seeing the boys again. Nevertheless I came down to the chapel next Sunday afternoon. There was no sign of any of them when the meeting began. But a few minutes later, there was a sudden commotion at the door.

'Yer said ter come,' shouted a large stout boy who was the obvious leader. He was flanked by a long lanky lad with hair straggling over his eyes, and after him came a gaggle of smaller boys.

Once again, I sat them down at the back. But it did not take me long to decide that this was a hopeless arrangement and that there was in fact a great gulf between the neat little children at the front and these lads. I therefore disrupted everyone for a second time, and took 'the gang' through into the big chapel. This was dangerous. There was too much space for them to play hide and seek in, and quickly I sat them down.

'If you come on Sundays,' I announced, 'we are going to make a huge model in here. This thing,' I said pointing to the central pulpit, 'is going to be a high mountain. This part down here' – I pointed at the flat platform covering the baptistry – 'is going to be a desert; and we are going to make tents for a huge camp-site here' – I indicated the far side of the chapel. Their eyes brightened, and questions began.

'Wot for?' demanded the fat boy.

'Because we are going to learn a true story of what happened at a place like that a long time ago.'

'Why?'

'Because what happened then affects us today.'

'How d'yer know wot 'appened if it's all that long ago?'

'Because this Book describes it all.' I held up my Bible and prepared to answer a barrage of criticism. But for the moment the fat boy was silenced by questions from the others.

'How'll we do the mountain?' shrilled a small lively lad. His mates did not wait for me to reply, but began a noisy discussion. They could get boxes from the shops. Someone knew where he could find old sacks. Another could bring wood. 'I'll have to get sand for the desert,' I put in. 'We'll get that,' they shouted. 'When can we start? Why wait till Sunday?'

But I was adamant: not till next Sunday. I knew that I needed at least a week to think out how to create this rashly conceived scheme for transforming the chapel into Mount Sinai and the wilderness. For the rest of the

44

first afternoon I shouted above the scuffles as I began the story of how the children of Israel came to be camping below Mount Sinai, and how Moses went up the mountain to receive the Ten Commandments.

It was not a whole week before I saw the gang again. As I walked down the street one evening, they rushed at me from the steps of one of the tenement houses.

'Can we bring the boxes round tomorrow night?' They could; and they did. Several helpers were busy inserting magazines into envelopes when the gang arrived with piles of cardboard boxes of all shapes and sizes. These they bundled through into the chapel, but were in no hurry to leave. They wandered round the hall, peered over the helpers' shoulders, picked up and examined magazines and anything else that lay about.

'Can we 'elp?' they asked.

The colour of their hands put paid to that and, at last, they reluctantly departed.

Next Sunday they arrived late again, causing the same disruption. This time I led them straight through to the chapel. They were eager to start on the model, but I insisted that first they should sit along the front pew and listen to the next instalment of the story. After that everyone rushed at the various tools, without thought of planning or preparation. I realised how much I was going to need help.

From then on the group was remarkably regular, except for Terry. He was not a close friend of the others, but lived next door to the fat leader, Dave, and his brother Colin. Terry was black-haired, blue-eyed and wild. He was beginning to be more interested in girls than in hanging about with the gang, and, as I soon learned, he was constantly in trouble because he would not go to school. He was the youngest of a family whose father had died. His older brothers were married and lived away from home, and although his mother did her best to cope with Terry, she went out cleaning soon after six am. Terry was therefore left to get himself to school . . . or not to. He had been punished; the Welfare

Officer had visited the home; letters arrived from the school; and at last he was due to go to Court. One day his mother, whom I had not seen before, stopped me and asked if I would speak for him. She was afraid that he would be sent away. It was my first experience of appearing in Court and I was as nervous as Terry. He was given a last chance, and for some weeks after that he did in fact go to school. On the evening after the Court case Terry appeared at the chapel door with a bouquet of expensive flowers, 'From Mum.' It was my first experience of the warm-hearted generosity of those people. If they wanted to do something for you they literally did not count the cost but would spend far more than they could afford, or than most of us would have done. In the same way I noticed that if youngsters had any money on them, most would cheerfully give their last penny away to a mate who needed it.

But to go back to the regular 'gang', Dave and Colin lived in one of the high houses down the street. Their mother, and her childless married sister, spoiled them both and loved to boast proudly about what they did and said. The father was a quiet elderly man who drove a furniture removal van. Dave's ambition, now long achieved, was to drive a heavy goods vehicle. His size and self-confidence had made him leader of the group, but already when I first met them he was beginning to lose his hold over the others who were in fact more adventurous than him. His second was Ernie, a very different type. He was the youngest of ten. His father had been disabled since the war and could not work. His mother went out to clean, besides having to cope at home in their basement flat, and was far too weary to do much about bringing up Ernie, who ran wild accompanied everywhere by his dog Sandy, whom he loved. Ernie for all his moods and waywardness was perhaps the most warm-hearted of them all.. His closest friend was not in fact Dave but Mick, who came from yet another type of background. He and his two younger brothers, whom we were soon to know, lived with hard-working parents in a secure family unit and had a number of relations living close by. There were no deep-seated problems in their home life.

This was not so for two more of the group. Les and Roy were the youngest of a family of fourteen. Their mother was the second wife, and the eldest children of the first wife's family were already almost middle-aged. Only Les and Roy and their two elder sisters were still at school when we met them. The mother worked hard; the father spent most of his time, when not working, in the pub getting 'nasty' drunk. On arrival home there was often violent trouble, and his main butt was poor Les – a stolid slow-thinking boy, who had had any self-confidence beaten out of him long ago by a father who would humiliate him in whatever ways he could. Not so Roy, the youngest. He was small, cheeky, and quick to get out of the way, and to leave the slower Les to face whatever trouble was coming. Roy loved animals and their backyard and shed usually held an assortment of his pets. He was also quick and good at working with his hands on any kind of woodwork or modelling, and it was he whom I first got to start on details of our Sinai model, the tents, the people and the golden calf.

Then there was Tortoise, so called for his odd way of walking. He had a creative turn of mind and enjoyed planning his particular part of the model. I also remember him spending happy hours designing a tree-house that would have man traps beneath it.

The last of the group but by no means the least, was John, otherwise known as Butch. He and Roy were the two youngest, hardly eleven yet. John lived close to the chapel with his parents, his older brother and three sisters. It was a two-storied terrace house, but the family lived upstairs apart from the two boys who had a bedroom on the ground floor. The rest of that floor was given up to the rag and bone trade. The father, a handsome stern man with gypsy blood, was a 'totter' and kept his stock in the house. John did not like going to bed before his older brother, because there were odd sounds from the heaps of waste stuff outside his bedroom, and an occasional rat would scamper by. The father was given to bouts of drinking, could be violent and was exceedingly strict with his children who were never allowed out late. Yet this was a family who grew up to do well, and all the children in their different ways had charm. At that time however John was still grubby, tousle-headed and very mischievous.

Inevitably with such a group, the pattern of our Sunday-school suffered a sea change. This became all the more evident when, very soon, the group's younger brothers-and-sisters-and-cousins-and-friends began to arrive. When I had previously asked children to come, none had responded; now, we could not keep them out! The young ones were not eligible to join the group in the big chapel, much to their disappointment, and it was vital that we should think out what to do with them, since they could not possibly integrate into the previous little ones' class. Should they be turned out? That would have been the simplest. But if we believed our Christian faith, we had to remember how our Lord treated children. He had cared about them, and exhorted us to do the same. Wasn't it important that we should try to think clearly about the patterns and content of our teaching? The first result of our difficulties was that the leader resigned. All his experience had been along traditional lines with children of church-going parents, and he genuinely and regretfully felt himself unable to cope with the type of our newcomers. That left the Sunday-school to a few of us who had never been trained nor had experience of Sunday-schools of any sort.

While this obviously presented difficulties, it also had its advantages in that we had no pre-conceived ideas of how to conduct Sunday afternoons any more than we assumed that children would necessarily behave in a conventional way. The riotous arrival of groups, therefore, did not dismay us. I suppose that one of the most dangerous pitfalls for the children of church-going parents is to assume that an outwardly respectable veneer and conformity are synonymous with Christianity. The inevitable result of this kind of thinking is to emphasise the importance of outward trappings and to confuse cultural patterns with basic principles that are essential to Christianity. Our dilemma was to find a way through this. If we imposed the patterns of traditional middle-class Sunday-schools, we would have been foisting an alien sub-culture on children whose life-style was totally different. Somehow we had to find ways of presenting Christian teaching that did not do violence to basic principles, but which would be meaningful to the type of children who confronted us.

Moreover, we had to avoid the error of mistaking the children's ignorance for lack of intelligence. As we soon discovered many of them had razor-sharp cockney wits and we could not hope to get away with muddled thinking without a shrill, and all too penetrating, interjective from one of them. One disastrous afternoon we took the whole Sunday-school to a children's anniversary service at another church. Nothing went badly wrong until the guest-speaker embarked on a somewhat whimsical explanation of the fruits of the Spirit (which in any case as yet held no meaning for our mob!).

'Now, what grows on an apple-tree? the speaker asked. A child from the home-church gave the correct answer; 'And on a pear-tree?' Again a child replied. 'And on a plum-tree?' This was too much. Dave raised his head and called, 'A lump of coal!' 'Shut up!' I hissed. 'Well,' he growled very audibly, 'a silly question deserves a silly answer, don't it?'

While we were grappling with these problems of how to teach our motley crowd, the model in the chapel was still taking shape. Mount Sinai, an erection over the pulpit of boxes and painted sacks, was striking in its splendour; a host of tents were appearing, and Roy and Tortoise fashioned animals and men in flowing robes. The Golden Calf was begun, and finally I decided that we should all make a detailed model of the Tabernacle. Only one thing was lacking. One Sunday the boys arrived dragging heavy sacks which they disgorged over the floor. The desert had appeared. I was delighted that they had been able to bring so much sand and wanted them to go and thank whichever parents or relatives had supplied it. I was still very green. It was not until I passed a nearby road works and saw the Council's heaps of sand that I had misgivings. It seemed an unfortunate outcome of teaching the Ten Commandments! And what was I to do when we reached the Eighth Commandment, 'Thou shalt not steal'? Should we shovel the sand back?

3: Can We 'ave a Club?

The request came from Dave and co. At first I brushed the idea aside as impossible, but they would not take 'No' for an answer. Every time I saw them they brought it up again, and I found myself beginning to discuss the idea with them, though still with the hope of putting an end to it. I should have known better: 'Just a little club' – 'just for us' – 'once a week', on and on they wheedled.

I still had hesitations. Would it be a right use of the chapel premises to allow a weekly club? Not long before, I would have been rigidly opposed to boys coming into a chapel, however disused, to enjoy themselves. But already my dogmatism was receiving a rude shake-up from these turbulent youngsters, and principles no longer appeared to be quite so sharply etched in black and white, when seen against a real life situation. For instance, how did one apply one's Christian faith in this particular situation? We had a large disused hall. The boys had only the streets and the dump (relic of the war) to play on. Already I was aware that there was no room in their own houses for them to meet and make a clutter. Was it right to keep our doors shut to them all the week, and then for an hour on Sundays to welcome them in, somewhat patronisingly perhaps, in order to teach them about God? Whatever we might *tell* them, what sort of God were we actually *showing* them? All the same, I went on arguing to myself. We had no adequate facilities. I knew nothing about youth clubs but even I could see that the hall and chapel were not cut out for such activities; besides, what sort of activities would be possible? Then again, any club would need helpers.

At some stage in my thinking, an idea began to emerge; could we build a boat? – not a model, but a boat that we could use. I suggested this to the boys, who were immediately full of enthusiasm. Next, I discussed the idea with John Mitrega and his wife Margaret. John was a splendid person. He was Polish, and had lost a foot fighting with the allied forces in the war. He had remained in England afterwards and had devoted himself to making false limbs for the disabled. His wife Margaret was English. I had met them through her sister, a ballet dancer who had become a Christian and through whom both John and Margaret had been led to commit their lives to Christ. As a first-class carpenter and craftsman, John was confident that he could construct a canoe if we obtained plans, and he was willing to teach the boys. Neither of us then appreciated the difficulties.

My next step was to make contact with the Youth Office, then situated in scrubby little rooms above a shoe-shop at the Junction. I came away with the promise of a small grant towards the cost of tools and material, and with information about where to obtain working plans for a wood structured, canvas covered, canoe. John did the preliminary work of getting the plans and ordering the wood and tools. Then I introduced him to the boys, who pored over the plans and understood nothing. Nor did they understand John's broken English. But everyone was excited, and when the wood was delivered, clamoured to begin. It was decided that the work should be done in the main chapel where there was plenty of room to store the timber and to assemble the sixteen-foot frame. It would not interfere with Mount Sinai or the desert and its camps. The trouble was that the boys had neither the patience nor self-control to work from plans with exact measurements. They wanted to rush in and do everything at once. To make the confusion worse, they all wanted the same tools at the same time, and those who failed to get them were apt to give up and disappear into the back reaches of the chapel to play a game of 'he'.

We were soon to find out how rare the quality of concentration was, and unhappily this is still true some twenty years later. Anything that does not yield quick results, soon palls. Another characteristic which we soon learnt to our cost, and which is still evident, is an almost universal carelessness with tools and materials. This was appalling to John, a craftsman to his fingertips and with a European peasant background. But though the first few weeks of boat-building must have been torment to him, he never gave in or lost his temper. Slowly he gathered round him a few of the boys who were genuinely interested in working with their hands, and the rest came and went and rushed around in the background. Obviously something and someone was needed to occupy these last. The 'someone' who appeared, and for some years remained one of our most dedicated helpers, was Ted Doe. At the time he was a bandsman in one of the Guards Regiments but he later went to a college of music and then played in the Bournemouth Symphony Orchestra. He had not much more skill at handwork than the boys, but he was prepared to learn, and above all, Ted had perseverance. It was this last quality and his genuine Christian concern that finally earned him the respect of hordes of youngsters who teased and tested him unmercifully in the coming months.

While Ted was trying to interest restless boys in balsa wood models, or was chasing after them when they commandeered the tools, Margaret Mitrega and I were facing problems in the school hall. The boys who were boat-building were continually sending one of their group out to the corner shop for sweets. Every time the door opened on to the street, two or three younger children would rush in. If the door remained unlocked, others would appear, and we would soon have a couple of dozen newcomers wandering around. Younger brothers and sisters from about six years old ran in and out, older boys and girls clamoured to join the boat-builders, and still older youths and girls nearing school-leaving age began to stroll in to have a look around. They were not allowed into the main chapel for fear of further disruption, but they did not want to go home. Couldn't they have something of their own to do in the school halls?

Once again events had overtaken us, and something clearly needed to be done. The boat-building had been started specifically for one group of boys, and we could not include a crowd of newcomers. Either we would have to drive these away, or we would have to adapt. We decided to adapt. After all we were not in the business of Youth Clubs. Our aim was primarily to tell and endeavour to show all who came our way that the gospel is still good news. If traditional Sunday-school methods were not effective, then we had better welcome in those who were now clamouring at our doors. And so the Thursday Club came into being.

Soon, Margaret and Brenda Mason, one of our helpers in the Sunday-school, were encouraging the girls and some boys to be busy with all sorts of crafts and talking while they worked. Ted had increased the size of his obstreperous group, many of whom evolved fascinating games in and out and round the pews. Jill, the physiotherapist who had been helping to despatch the magazine, nobly volunteered to take the youngest children into the back room to make models, paint pictures and play games. I was left 'spare', since my role was to be at the door whenever children arrived and if possible to channel them into one or other of the groups, or at least to try to prevent chaos.

It was at this stage that we began to charge the children threepence (in 'old pence') to come in for the evening. I had already come to the conclusion, from which I have never wavered, that it is a thoroughly bad principle to give children everything without receiving some token from them, although we always made exceptions where we knew of children who genuinely could not get even threepence from their parents. I collected the pennies in a coffee tin. To begin with the children also got an orange drink and a bun for their 'subs'. We gave these out at the end of the evening when everyone assembled in the hall, and sat almost silent in rows. I said 'grace' and helpers handed round the refreshments. But as the club grew and we started a canteen, this custom ended except for the little ones who still had a free orange drink after they had listened to a Bible story at the end of their evening.

Jill in the back room had by far the worst 'pitch'. It was a throughway to the yard and the toilet. Boys were continually rushing past, and a favourite trick was to bolt the door when someone was outside. When he could not re-enter he would crash on the door and shout until Jill stopped whatever she was doing, and went to let him in. While she was thus occupied, the little ones would upset paints or run away to play, and inquisitive older children would come in to see what was going on and would delightedly take over paints, crayons and paper. Clearly something would have to be done to control the situation.

At the other end of the age range there was also need. The lordly older brothers and friends would not demean themselves by joining young ones, but were demanding why they could not have a 'senior club'. It was the same old story: 'just for them', 'only once a week', 'only a little club'.

In our ignorance, we had in fact begun something which was supplying a hitherto largely unrecognised need. As I now know, the great majority of youth clubs and uniformed organisations, whether secular or church-based, had inherited the structures of an earlier generation and were still primarily 'activity based'. Children joined secular clubs to take part in organised sport and specialist activities and the clubs were run on authoritarian, disciplined lines which gave little scope for them as social meeting places. Church-based youth clubs, for their part, usually met in part of the church premises, which obviously limited their activities. It also required a strict code of behaviour, since too much noise or horseplay might annoy others using the building, and smoking could not be tolerated. In any case, they catered primarily for children of church-going parents, and others who came were usually expected to attend Sunday-school.

Most of these clubs had a formal epilogue, which was compulsory for everyone. They did good work within their own spheres, but the generation growing up in the early sixties was dropping out from traditional youth works and hanging around on street corners, in parks and in derelict old houses. They did not want the organised sports and activities, but they did still want a place where they could meet together, and they, no less than the 'conformists', desperately needed help in developing interests, being introduced to constructive rather than destructive ways of spending time, and in beginning to discover wider horizons on life for themselves. How best to do this is still, twenty years later, a million dollar question for the nation. But in the days I am talking about one thing was certain. To the 'unclub-bables', the unstructured and untraditional basis in which we struggled to keep up with events rather than laying down the rules first (we were in any case too ignorant ourselves to be able to do that) was like a magnet. Every week more youngsters arrived on our doorstep.

For a while we went on week by week taking things as they came. But soon we had to face the fact that if we were to cater for all the age groups already present with us we would have to set aside an evening for the little ones on their own, and another for the 'seniors'. This raised the whole question of priorities with regard to our use of the chapel, and what in fact was the proper use for it. Already this had changed from our original intention of simply running the magazine there. True, our helpers did still struggle through two evenings of magazine work amid interruptions from youngsters pounding on the door and asking to come in. There were new difficulties too with having to store our stock and equipment out of reach of exploring hands.

We also still held our weekly women's meeting on one evening, but having recognised the wisdom of changing this to an afternoon, we did this as soon as we could. On one of our first afternoon meetings we persuaded Mrs Lloyd-Jones to come down and speak. From those very early months she has in fact never failed to give encouragement and help or to show an active interest in what has been going on. I remember meeting her at the station and escorting her through our side streets. When we came in sight of the chapel we saw several very small children with hands above them grasping our letter box and pulling themselves up to peer through. Others who could not get a handhold had their eyes glued to the crack of the door. It was a daunting sight for any speaker, the more so as some of these little people slipped into the hall and sat down with our few old ladies. Mrs Lloyd-Jones is however one of those rare people who is real wherever she is and for whom people are themselves, not types or classes, and that meeting lives in my memory as one of the best we had. Afterwards when some of the boys' Sunday group pushed in on their way from school to see what was going on, they took Mrs Lloyd-Jones round the Sinai Desert, kindly explaining the story in case she had not heard it.

Besides putting a strain upon our use of the chapel, these increasing activities were encroaching on my own work. It became more difficult to spend time writing, and the research that I had been doing at the British Museum languished. When I went down to the chapel in the day time, intending to shut myself in the back 'office', I was usually seen on my way there and soon there would be thumps on the door. Perhaps I should have ignored them, though probably the door would have caved in; as it was I spent a good many hours talking to the twos and threes who wandered in.

I was encouraged to think that this was not just time-wasting (as some people told me), when a friend from the Wycliffe Bible Translators came to visit me one day and I took her to see the chapel. She and her husband had spent over a year living among a primitive tribe while they studied the tribe's spoken language and reduced it to writing for the first time. While we talked, there was a bang on the outer door. Three teenage girls came in. I knew them a little, but had not met them on their own before. They wanted to look at everything, and not just to look. They opened cupboards and drawers and carefully fingered their contents. They picked up the various objects on my desk and pulled out books from the shelves. As they did so they asked questions. These ranged from the commonplace: What were we doing here? Why did we have a magazine? to the more personal: How old were we? Why don't we smoke? You don't swear — why not? What are you telling people the Bible for, what has all that got to do with us?

When at last they left us, my friend remarked that she felt that she had been back among her tribe for the afternoon, since this was exactly the sort of thing that had happened while she had lived with them. Moreover, one of the basic principles of their missionary work was to live alongside the people and to encourage them to come in and out of their home and ask questions. But it was, she emphasised, far more demanding to do this than simply to hold meetings at stated times. I was to find out what she meant.

Up till now, I had made the bus journey between Kensington and Clapham Junction several times a week. But I was spending more and more time at the chapel, and I began to wonder whether I should try to find somewhere to live in that neighbourhood. It would not be easy since the housing problem in Battersea was acute. But I began to see the issue as one that would confirm, or not, whether I should go on spending time among the people and children, or whether I should give it all up. If there was nowhere for me to live it would indicate that I was not intended to spend more time there. I made this a matter of much prayer.

One day I was told that the top flat was becoming vacant in a three-storey house about ten minutes walk from the chapel, between the Junction and the Common. The house had seen better days, as had the road. In late Victorian times middle-class families had lived there, and a plaque on the wall of one stated that the boys' story writer G A Henty had occupied it. Now most of the houses were divided into three or more flats. Number 43 had a common hall and staircase, both shabby. The three flats had no separate front doors and one walked up through the middle flat to reach the top, which was on two levels. It, too, was shabby and the kitchen fittings consisted of a cold tap and a sink, while the tiny bathroom had an ineffective geyser. But there were two pleasant bedrooms, and a large low-ceilinged attic room which I decided would make an attractive sitting room. The rent was negligible, and I took the flat. Friends helped me to redecorate, and I brought bits of furniture from my parents' home to supplement what I already had. I also bought a gas cooker, and chose crisp cottage-style curtain materials. The people below me, an elderly widow and her daughter, could not have been more helpful or pleasant, and when I moved in a new chapter in my life had begun.

Confirmed in my belief that we should continue working with the children, I discussed with helpers the next urgent steps to be taken. We began an early morning prayer meeting twice a week. We did not choose the time, seven a.m. because we enjoyed getting up early or because we necessarily saw peculiar merit in starting the day in this way. Some of the helpers travelled several miles to reach the chapel before going to work. But it was becoming hard to fit in anything more in the evenings, and there were so many interruptions at the chapel then that early morning seemed best. There were usually about half a dozen of us, and together we brought before the Lord all our many needs. Neither the magazine nor the other project had any financial backing, and above all we needed wisdom to know how to proceed with the various works that were springing up spontaneously round us in the old building, and, most important, we needed wisdom in how to communicate with both young and old.

We decided that as soon as possible we should have an evening for little children of ten and under, from six o'clock to eight. They would then no longer be banished to the back room, but would have the school hall for games, and before going home we would have them sitting down while we told them a Bible story. This pattern, and even the day – Tuesday – has in fact continued ever since. To begin with we had problems in that as soon as the older children realised that the 'Club' was open on another evening, they too wanted to come in and this required a determined doorkeeper.

'I got ter come in too – Mum says I 'ave to go with my sister,' a twelve-year-old would expostulate.

Or 'Honest, I'm only ten. I know I look big – all my family are big,' a thirteen-year-old would gaze innocently at me.

Or, just, '*Please* – we will be good – just this time!'

Sometimes I relented, and usually regretted it as the bigger children wanted to take over games and activities. After the story, it was time to go home. But it was not easy to get everyone away. They were like slippery eels, slinking under tables and hiding, or running from room to room. If someone was not guarding the door, as fast as one batch went out another lot would run in again.

The original Thursday evening club continued and between sixty and seventy children came regularly. We had the same problem at the door as on Tuesdays, only it was the little ones who would try to slip in unnoticed. When they were rejected they would sit in the gutter outside, apparently forlorn but in fact alert, waiting for the door to open to make another dash. I was usually in charge of the door, and began to carry about with me a large strap-handled handbag. Into this I crammed my coffee tin of pennies, all the odds and ends which children asked me to look after for them, extra table tennis balls, darts, and anything else that I found lying about. The bag became an essential part of my equipment. There was to come a time when I insisted on all weapons being put in it before the owner came in and I would clank about with a formidable arsenal.

We had acquired a table tennis table and, somewhat dangerously, a darts board. We also started cookery in the dreadful back premises. Our facilities consisted of an old cooker and a sink; a tap already existed. A kitchen table completed our fittings. In spite of the total lack of 'ideal home' atmosphere, these sessions proved very popular, and many more wanted to take part than the 'kitchen' would hold, so that there were constant interruptions from the unlucky ones who had been banished, besides the usual through traffic to the outside toilet.

Some time later we were visited by an Education Authority Inspector who toured youth clubs. She arrived immaculately dressed with, I recall, a double row of artificial pearls and well groomed hairstyle. It was on a Thursday, and when she had seen the crowd perched on and round the table in the hall either working at some craft or running away with equipment, and had navigated a course round the table tennis, avoiding the darts, she arrived in the doorway of the cookery class. Some years later I was to know her better, and she recalled with relish the scene that had confronted her. It was raining that evening, and water dripped through the roof on to the table where children vigorously stirred their concoctions; a kettle steamed on the stove and youngsters crowded round it for warmth; boys ran in and out bound for the toilet; others peered over the girls' shoulders into the cooking bowls before being chased out by 'the Cook', scarlet faced, with hair awry, and flour on her face.

As yet our only heating, apart from the cooking stove

and the ancient gas fire in my 'office', was the lethal oil stove, which we banished as soon as we could. We had no chairs, just the victorian Sunday-school forms, the chair in my back room and the top of my desk. I did not see this lack of equipment as any advantage at the time. But looking back I am convinced that it was one reason for the children identifying themselves so much with that old building. They felt that it was theirs in a way they never would have done had everything been laid on for them and expensive equipment laid out for them to misuse without thought. As it was, they brought bits and pieces round to the 'Club' themselves; they began to paint the walls with us; they repaired rotten floorboards; and were soon to embark on more ambitious projects. But that was when the senior club got going.

We began this in response to the continued demands and pleading of older boys and girls. In fact it was Les and Roy's older sisters who were most insistent. Iris, tall, dark, moody and good looking, was in her last year at school. Pauline, small, blonde and bright-eyed like Roy, was already at work. They used to be sent round for their brothers when they were late, except when their father had come back from the pub in a particularly nasty mood. Then he would stumble round to us himself in order to humiliate Les and knock him about in front of everyone. In spite of Iris and Pauline's entreaties, I hesitated for some time before opening the senior club. We had so little equipment; the place was unsuitable; and I had been warned that a previous youth club up the road had come to a smashing end, and that ours would too. On the other hand, there were those pathetic groups outside.

What finally made the senior club possible was that Rosemary volunteered to help with running it. She already knew the building from having come down regularly to work on the magazine, but her evening at the senior club was the beginning of an association that caused her eventually to give up her prospects of

62

promotion in physiotherapy, to take a part-time job in what was then a run-down geriatric hospital near the Junction, and to pack into the rest of the day more hours' work than most workers do in their full working day. In spite of the heavy load of work however, it has to be said that she has survived and is still working with me and helping me to recall this tale.

The first seniors came in on a Monday evening. With a smaller group the dim rather dingy hall looked even less inviting. The oil heater threw out heat for a circumference of about two feet, and then there was only cold air. But it did not seem to matter. It was a place where they could meet together. They huddled in a tight circle round the oil stove, and I got the first inkling of the ceaseless chatter of those who do not read or write or have any intellectual outlet. They just talk.

We made only one concession to the senior boys. We decided that we must buy them some sort of snooker table. We saw an advertisement of a half-size slate bedded table, with a sectional oak top which when fitted had formed a Victorian dining table, and with a donation we bought it. That table was to prove marvellous value for the fifty pounds we spent on it, which included a set of balls and several cues. All these years later it is still in regular use, though it has been re-covered more than once by 'Lenny the Pill' who first wandered into our Monday Club in those days.

To begin with the boys who came in on a Monday evening were those who had already got to know us and had asked for their own evening. They lived locally and some had younger brothers and sisters who came on Tuesdays and Thursdays. But soon they were bringing friends, and others who lived in nearby streets came in. Needless to say, the fact that boys were meeting in the chapel brought in girls. They too, to begin with, lived locally and already knew most of the boys.

During the first winter of that senior club, Rosemary and I spent most Monday evenings either sitting round our evil smelling oil stove in a corner of the Sunday-school hall or in my back room, jammed among a solid wedge of youths and girls. The group was by no means static. One of the first characteristics we noticed was the inability of the youngsters to stay at anything for any length of time: they would drift off to play some game for a short while, then back to the group, then away to something else, and back again, and so on through the evening.

We listened much more than we talked. I have never understood why women are accused of gossiping more than men: certainly among our crowd it has always been the boys who do most of the talking. It was brought home to me that winter that *talking*, not reading or writing, was their potent means of communication. They were not interested in books. Someone might take a volume from the shelf in my room and open it, but on seeing a page of solid print would quickly shut it again. They would look at a tabloid, and boys and girls of working age would pore over a comic. But nothing more; and we soon learnt that a good many had difficulty in reading at all, and in writing (something that is still true twenty years later).

If by any extraordinary chance anyone received a letter or postcard, then it was brought to the club and passed round. Everyone would study it with the greatest interest. Later on when we began taking children away we got used to this, and to the ignorance of almost all of them about how to write and address, what sort of stamp was necessary, and even whether letters were delivered on Sundays. In these more sophisticated days, twenty years later, all this is still true, and many teenagers have an idea that the more stamps you put on a letter the quicker it will go! Most preferred school detention to doing homework and we got the impression that after a while schools gave them up as a bad job. In any case, the youngsters had little encouragement at home to respect school authority, or even in some cases to go to school. 'Mum needed me at home,' was not always just an excuse. And, when a child had not felt like going to school, his mother would often oblige by writing a note saying that he was ill. So much for school authority.

The hours we spent listening that first winter were the best education we could have had for getting inside these young people's lives and to some extent inside their minds. Most of us have little idea how much our thought forms are moulded by our background and environment. We tend to assume that English people in England speak the same language and mean the same things when they use identical words. But I was soon disabused of this notion. These lads and girls used very few words and what they said was direct, with no covering up the meaning in wrappings of polite or oblique suggestions.

I soon realised that it was important for us to understand this, and that these people could take straight talk which would have deeply offended many brought up in 'polite' circles. Sometimes, when I had shouted particularly loudly at one or another to 'stop it' – whatever 'it' was – I was afraid that I had been too fierce and that they would not return. I need not have worried. Their childhoods had not been spent hearing, 'Now darling, leave that and come to mummy,' followed by a reason. What they had heard bawled was: 'Stop that! – Shut up you little b—!,' 'Here you! – Get up!' and so on. Communications had been almost mono-syllabic, with no reasons given. Descriptive adjectives and adverbs were also missing, except for four letter epithets which abounded. Those were in fact so much part of everyday life that often when I told them how unnecessary and ugly swearing was they had not noticed they were doing so. Another thing was that quiet talk was at a premium. They were used to shouting at one another and being shouted at, and literally did not know how to whisper. I remember suffering many times later when we had a group with us either at church or at some equally solemn and silent occasion; a child would suddenly come out with quite a serious remark or question, but always in a loud, penetrating voice.

As we listened to that vehement, shrill talk we began to realise something of the constant tensions that made up home life and their relationships with others. They were growing up amid adults who alternated between shrill violent clashes and feuds, and just as shrill bouts of hilarity. There was little attempt at self-control, and – *no tenderness*. A man lost his temper, and hit another. A woman swore like a fishwife one moment and was laughing five minutes later. Small wonder that the children shouted and swore, fought one minute and were good mates again the next.

While the youngsters huddled in the warmth and talked, almost without knowing it their hands would be busy tearing something up, senselessly cutting, breaking and destroying it, even if it was only their own pencil or box of matches. For they were as careless with their own things as with the belongings of others. We would see them hold the end of their belts or scarves in the fire just for the fun of watching them burn. If they tore their clothes, they would very likely rip them still further and deliberately destroy them rather than think of mending them. They delighted in poking the ancient gas fire until the filaments broke, and when we warmed ourselves with cups of tea would pour the dregs over the oil burner. They were not being deliberately destructive so much as working out an aimlessness that we soon recognised as being inherent in their lives.

Even in those days of the early sixties the youngsters who wandered in from the street corners, alleys and empty houses, appeared to be without sense of purpose. They knew little of hopes or ideals, and their only ambition was to make money as quickly and easily as they could.

'What's the use of waiting till you're twenty-one,' observed Paul about someone who had money to come, 'we may be dead before then.' And he nearly was – from drugs. That boy had never known his father; his mother had many men in and out of the house. Paul was exceptionally gifted in drawing and design, and through personal contacts we arranged an interview for him with the art department of an advertising agency. But we had not yet understood that for many it was more than they could cope with to get themselves organised and arrive by themselves for an interview in an unknown, alien world. He never arrived, though he started out. Later that day he was picked up, stoned, and taken to the old Charing Cross Hospital.

The temptation for those about to leave school was to take any dead-end job rather than go for training or apprenticeship. The dead-end job offered more immediate money, and they were not going to think further ahead. What they wanted was money in their pockets to spend, and enough to put down in deposit on a scooter. But even that ambition had little bite to it. One evening a lad would come in full of excitement: he had got his new scooter. Everyone would rush out to see it, hoping for an illegal ride round the block. A week or two later I would ask how the bike was going. He would shrug, carelessly: 'Oh, it got smashed up.' It was finished: he had forgotten.

They were not all like this of course. Bob comes to mind at once. He was John's older brother, a good-looking, quietly spoken lad who used to come in regularly with his girl, Val. Both were soon to leave school. Now they are married, with their own family and house, but then they had little money and they desperately wanted somewhere to meet where they could talk and be together. Hence the club. Bob's father could be, and often was, harsh but without his insistence that his son should do a proper job Bob might well have drifted like the others. As it was, he was apprenticed as a plasterer, and had the guts to stick at it and Val stuck to him even though there was little money for several years.

Bob's cousin Peter was also apprenticed to the same firm, but he had been over-indulged all his life by a doting mother, and his hardworking craftsman father was not strong enough to stand up to mother and son. Catastrophe was soon to follow; meanwhile Peter did not at all like hard work for low wages. Gerry was bone idle. His older brothers had a coal business, and from time to time Gerry worked with them, but most of his days were spent round the betting shops. The result was, and still is, that sometimes he rides high, with money to burn. At other times he is broke. A few years ago he was conspicuously absent from his old friend Peter's wedding. 'Where's Gerry?' I asked, for everyone else from those early days seemed to be there. Peter's mother explained. He was skinned, and had not got a suit to come to the party in. He was too ashamed to come without a suit. Not so 'Lenny the Pill'. He had not been invited, but as I left I met him ambling along in scruffy jeans: 'Hear there's a party,' he mumbled. Mick on the other hand had, quite exceptionally, thought out his future with care. His widowed mother had brought him up and he was determined to get on. He became an electrical apprentice and in due course became an electrician with the LEB. He bought his own house, but when I last saw him he was going to emigrate to Australia. He like many of the others had a lot of loyalty. When Peter got into trouble and was in prison, Mick, Bill and even Gerry used to spend one evening a week with Peter's mother.

One very evident characteristic of most boys and girls was their lack of self-control. They lived by impulse. You would see them talking, playing some game, even working sensibly when suddenly someone would say something to annoy. In a moment, there was the start of a fight. But get between them in that one moment, and the whole thing would die and in a minute or two might never have been. It was as senseless as that. It made for an existence that alternated between aimless lethargy and sudden tempestuous•bouts of misdirected energy, that all too easily ended in violence and damage. *That* was its danger. The thought only came later, after the razor, the knife or the brick had been used, so that one needed to be alert to intervene in that one crucial moment before trouble could brew.

Trouble of that sort did not in fact worry us during the first winter of the club. All that we had to contend with were the odd flare-ups with fists, and these were quickly quelled by some of the others; or, outbursts of wild spirits, particularly at closing time, which sent lads careering into the chapel, hurdling among the pews, swarming up pillars into the gallery and balancing on the railing, whooping and shouting: 'Catch us if you can!' Usually Bill was the leader. Sandy-red haired and hot-eyed, he reminded me of *Tiger Tim* in the old comic. Many predicted a bad end for him. Boys had only to dare him to something, and Bill would be making the attempt. Already he was fascinated by bikes and cars, and was getting himself a job training as a car mechanic. His stepfather, also in the motor trade, was seeing to this. During the next years there were often ructions at home, but the stepfather never abandoned Bill, however many troubles he got into, usually for mad fast driving and for one disastrous period when he got in tow with, and was fascinated by, a group of habitual drug-takers. Unlike some of these, Bill was no criminal at heart and today he has put on weight, is a steady married man who dotes on his small son.

I also have another picture of Bill, roaring up a remote Welsh mountain pass in his Mini-Cooper, and later that day leading a group of his mates in a wild chase up precipitous, dangerous crags, deaf to our shouts of warning.

'What on earth did you do that for?' I stormed, when at last they got down safely. 'You could have killed them all!'

'I was only following a sheep,' said Bill, somewhat shaken when he looked up to where they had been. 'I thought it was bound to know the way.'

I remember too the times that Bill has come out at any hour of day or night to help if our minibus had gone wrong and never accepting any payment. 'You do things for us. I do this for you.'

They were carelessly generous. If they had something, most would want to share it. And they were ready to help us keep that old building habitable. Had we been paid workers, and the building a council-run club, I doubt if we should have had the same assistance. For that matter we should not, in a material sense, have needed it. But as it was, we never lacked. When part of the ceiling fell in just before the children's Christmas party, smothering our preparations in clouds of plaster dust, Bob and his uncle were there immediately and the new ceiling was up just as the children arrived. Ernie, proud of becoming a plumber's mate helped with the installation of pipes for overhead gas heaters when we could bear the cold no longer. Mick and another Bill were soon able to attend to electrical work for us, while a number of younger lads painted over the dark chocolate walls, and spilled a good deal of paint on the floors. When they had finished I thought the place looked bright and cheerful. I was a bit daunted when a friend remarked it looked like a British Rail refreshment room.

Jim, or rather two Jims, took charge of our maintenance. One, an architect friend from Westminster Chapel, was to give much time over the next years to the practical work of keeping that building standing, and his chief ally was one of the older boys, also called Jim. The latter was a natural philosopher who would spend hours discussing life with us and questioning us closely about the Christian gospel. He was a fiercely proud boy who, when we first knew him, felt humiliated and ashamed of having been put on probation. It was he who summed up the misconception of so many: 'What has Christianity got to do with me?' he demanded one evening, 'Christians are *middle-class*. They wear collars. I'm working class, and I'm never going to wear a collar.' Could anything be further away from the biblical narrative that the *common* people heard Jesus gladly? Yet, looking around that area, it was obvious

70

that people were not hearing him, and that most *church goers* were concentrated further out, in middle-class suburban areas.

In between argument and discussion, Jim would go round the building with hammer and nails. Many of the floor-boards were rotten, and with hard use were now becoming dangerous. It was he too who designed and erected a huge wooden bar to be let down across the street door and fitted into metal slots, to keep the hordes outside from pushing the door in. I think that he got his idea from seeing films of besieged mediaeval fortresses. But it was effective. So was his re-roofing venture. I went into the lean-to we called the kitchen one evening to find stars shining where the leaking roof had been. Jim and his mates had taken the roof right off. They worked half the night to put a new one in place, which they later sealed liberally with pitch. 'It's all right – it's ours,' they declared as they heaved in a block of pitch big enough to resurface a stretch of motorway. I had my doubts, but by then it was steaming and bubbling.

One of Jim's mates was a giant known as Legs, who went about in a black leather coat emblazoned with a crimson eagle. For a while he was 'away', that is in prison. On his first morning out, he was at a loose end with nowhere to go and nothing to do so he came and banged on our door. He wandered round for a while, then said severely: 'That back door ain't safe – someone might break in.' I agreed, but pointed out the battering it got from those outside. 'I'll make you a new one,' he said. And he did.

If they could often be willing to give, they could also often take. 'Nicking' was an everyday habit. They even took things from their friends, and expected others to do the same. When they discovered something was missing they would simply shrug and forget it. In their book, that was life: easy come, easy go. There was no disgrace or shame attached to stealing and being caught. It was a big game. If you got away with booty from

Woolworths, or one of the other Clapham Junction stores, then it was something to boast about. All the same I found that the bag I carried around was increasingly used as a depository for other people's belongings which they gave me for safe keeping. It did not occur to them that I might make off with anything. A lad with some skill as a pick-pocket gave me his mother's money to mind one evening. 'Count it,' I said when I returned it to him. 'Wot for?' he replied. 'You've 'ad it, ain't yer?'

To some extent the building was already becoming more of a haven, even home, to a number of the youngsters than their own homes. Someone was nearly always there if they were in trouble, while at home parents were often out at work or in the pub. They arrived with cuts that needed washing, troubles to be sorted out, and some, locked out from their own homes, wanting somewhere to come in. On occasion it was also a refuge from family rows and tensions when they became unbearable. One night a boy rushed in with an armful of broken pieces of wood. He had rescued these from the piano which his father was smashing in a drunken frenzy, and he dared not go home again for a while. It was hardly surprising that that same boy was later in trouble for setting fire to someone else's property.

At the other end of the 'respectability scale', there were boys who came because everything was kept so neat and spotless at home that they were not allowed to bring any friends into the house or to make any untidy mess. This particular need has increased with the greater affluence of the past years, but it was on the way even then. It also became obvious to us very soon that most of the lads virtually brought themselves up after the age of about ten. There were of course exceptional family groups, but there was no question of the majority going out with their parents, or of parents introducing children to a variety of interests or trying to expand their horizons. Instead, the boys tended to depend for their society, their security and for their activities and interests entirely on the rest of their gang. They were in fact all whistling in the dark together, and often they had little or no meaningful dialogue or relationship with any adult – parents or teachers.

This was not so true of the girls. If they have hardly been mentioned in the last pages, it is because they were so obviously less dominant than the boys. Indeed, a great lesson to us was that the attitude of boy to girl in that society was mediaeval, primeval perhaps, compared with the already more 'liberated' middle classes. Boys would order a girl out to go and buy 'fags' or sweets for them – and the girls would go. If their lordships wanted a game of table tennis while girls were playing, they would expect to take over and the girls, apart from a few squeals, would acquiesce. A few were more independent in their attitude, and one or two like Val who already had steady boyfriends had somewhat different attitudes, but by and large the others accepted a subservient role as the norm. They had come in the first place because of the boys. There was nothing else to attract them in the dingy, chilly premises, and boys remained the focus of their whole being all the time. With the boys it was different. They enjoyed horse-play with the girls, but they would go off to play some tough game or become involved in argument or discussion and forget girls altogether for a while, even shouting at them to 'shut up' when feminine shrieks and giggles tried to distract them.

When we closed at night and the last were driven out, boys and girls departed in a noisy throng which spilled across the road. Only a few paired off. One such couple was Paul and Lenny's sister, Val. They made a striking couple, both tall and slim, Paul very blonde and Val with long dark hair. When, later, I left the building I would often pass them pressed together under the shadowy railway arches, surrounded by debris of waste ground, with a grimy, graffiti-scarred wall behind. Imprisoned in that sordid ugliness, they seemed to epitomise the loneliness and hopelessness of some of the youngsters.

For those first months most of the older lads who came into the club affected Mod styles, so far as they identified with any style. They were meticulously clean, and they tended towards sharp-pointed shoes, drainpipe trousers, and carefully combed hair style. One night, however, there was a bang on the outer door, followed by a pause. I went over and opened it, and the apparition on the doorstep came into view. It had a mop of shoulder-length hair; black leather jacket; open-necked shirt with red kerchief knotted round the throat; skin tight jeans decorated with metal studs down the seams; heavy studded belt, and boots from one of which protruded a workmanlike knife.

'Can I come in?' the youth asked.

'Can you behave?'

He nodded and I opened the door wider. Beckoning into the darkness behind, he stalked into the old building – to be followed, in single file like Indian braves, by sixteen more long-haired, belted and booted youths. Silence fell among our nattily dressed Mods and the smaller fry. The Rockers had arrived.

4: Going to 'Whales'

The banner consisting of part of an old white sheet, emblazoned with red-painted letters, was nailed inside the club porch for days before our first camp set off.

During the months after the club began, when numbers and clubs were continually increasing, our first group had sometimes felt neglected. They would like to have kept 'the club' and everything that went on there, to themselves. I could sympathise with their feeling to some extent, and tried to make it clear to them that as our first friends, they did have a special place and we were not going to overlook them. But this needed to be demonstrated in some practical way. The canoe was not finished and had had to be stored in the gallery for a while because too many boys swarmed round it and hindered rather than helped John. So we could not hope that year to let the original lads sail it. How about taking them away for a week?

Family holidays were still comparatively rare in those streets twenty years ago. There were a few day trips to the coast when Dad took his holiday, but apart from that, fishing in the pond on the Common or the Fun Fair at Battersea Park were the chief outlets during weekends and summer holidays. Locally, there were the dumps to play on, and the river wharves near by to explore somewhat dangerously. But for most children the country was something you passed through without paying much attention, as you sat in a train or bus on the way to the seaside. I was beginning to understand, too, how parochial their outlook was. Battersea was their 'parish' and anything outside that was strange territory. Even the other end of Battersea was different.

Only in the little area round the Junction were they really at home and secure. To suggest going camping in the country would therefore be an adventure.

More than that, it would be good for them to get out of 'man-made', 'man-centred' surroundings and be in a natural environment among hills and forests, and under broad skies not hemmed in by houses. We were not so naive as to think that this would of itself bring them to a belief in God. But at least it would give city-orientated lads an awareness of an altogether bigger dimension in life than they had yet experienced, and with natural creation on all sides it would, we hoped, stimulate their thinking of a supreme Creator.

Having decided to take the boys away, the next question was where to go. At least this was hardly a question for me. I realised almost at once that I would like to take them to one of the most beautiful and remote valleys in mid-Wales where my friends John and Mari have a sheep farm. They had recently built a new farmhouse and were letting the old house be used in the summers by Christian friends who needed a holiday. With the other helpers' agreement, I wrote to John and Mari to ask whether we might use the old house for a week, and bring tents for the boys to sleep in. It was a great testimony to their warmth of heart and devotion to all that they believed the Lord would have them do, that they agreed to have a bunch of wild city kids on a hill farm, where every blade of grass is precious and where careless damage can so easily be done, and can result in harm to livestock as well as to fences, gates and the like.

John and Mari were not the only generous friends who helped bring about that first camp. Dr Margery Blackie who first took me to Westminster Chapel had a great friend, Musette Majendie of Hedingham Castle, who devoted much time to the Scout movement. They were both personal friends of mine and were interested in hearing about our club efforts. They were essentially generous people and one day they announced that they would like to give us a present of two new tents.

One very hot evening in June, Musette came down to the old chapel building to deliver the tents and to give us a lesson in how to put them up. Mercifully, Rosemary had done some camping and knew her way about the tangle of ropes and sacks of poles. I knew nothing, having never camped in my life except in India with an army of servants to put the tents up and prepare an elaborate meal. The group of boys who had come in to share this lesson, as usual wanted to rush at everything without first listening to what they should do. Everyone except our group of prospective campers was locked out, but throughout the 'training' session we had an audience. They stood on one another's shoulders on the pavement outside and peered in through the high chapel windows.

Under Musette's redoubtable command, a tent was laid out on the ground in front of the pulpit where the Sinai Desert had, until recently, been located. The boys were marshalled into some sort of order, and with Musette working alongside them they did actually listen and learn. Afterwards they were directed to unwind a long hessian roll, and Musette demonstrated exactly how they were to dig the latrine and erect the canvas. She also reminded us that we must carry spades for this operation. The air was breathless and dusty; the western sun poured in; Musette, in full Scouts' uniform including hat, never flagged. 'I bet she ain't arf 'ot,' gasped one of the boys as he wiped his sweating brow, ' – and in that 'at too!'

'She's got 'er 'at on, cos she's a real lidy,' replied his mate severely.

'A real lidy' was the general verdict of the boys as they gave Musette a warm and noisy send-off later that night.

Another generous friend was John Raynar, a solicitor who was involved with us in the magazine's affairs. He insisted on hiring *two* minibuses for our expedition, which was planned to consist of twelve or thirteen boys,

John and Margaret Mitrega, Ted Doe, Rosemary and me. John and Rosemary had both driven minibuses before (John was coming with us for the first weekend and returning to work on Sunday night).

True to our principle, and because we had no financial grants, we charged the boys but made it the minimal sum of three pounds to include everything, in order that those in most need should not be put off. Excitement built up as the day approached. In spite of all the years they had been at school, they were not sure where Wales was. Was it a foreign country? Did they need passports? Did the people speak English? In point of fact the valley to which we were going was totally Welsh-speaking and the inhabitants, including our host John, had difficulty in expressing themselves in English.

A day or two before our departure, when we were busy buying supplies, troubles began. Two boys backed out without explanation. We were still too ignorant to realise the panic that could set in, even among seemingly tough boys, as the reality of leaving their own surroundings for the first time approached. And in these instances they had little help from parents in overcoming their fears. 'They've chickened out,' was the scornful verdict of the rest of the party. Then, on the day before we went, Dave and his brother Colin had a fight in the basement area outside their home. Dave gave a mighty punch, with all his considerable weight behind it, missed Colin and his hand and arm crashed through the glass window behind. He severed the nerves of two fingers and had to have stitches from his wrist to his elbow. That put an end to his coming away, or his brother. Now we had only nine boys left. On the morning of our departure, when John and Rosemary drove the vehicles to the club building at eight o'clock as arranged, we found only eight lads waiting there with a few somewhat dishevelled mums. The boys looked small and white-faced. It was nearly an hour later by the time the vans were loaded and the eight boys had got in.

There was still no sign of Ernie. John, youngest of the party, rushed off. At last, hesitantly, Ernie appeared at the corner with John, and stopped. He looked as if he was about to run away again. He was dressed in his usual patched jeans and shapeless pullover and appeared only to have a carrier bag by way of luggage. Suddenly, he made up his mind, squared his shoulders, and with a disarming shy smile joined his mates in the van. We were ready to go.

We reckoned that we had a journey of two hundred and forty miles ahead of us. The first hundred miles passed uneventfully enough as we drove first along the M1 and then turned off on to major roads that took us towards the A5. The minibuses had little acceleration and the clutch on one of them was worn. But it was only when we were beginning to think of stopping for a picnic lunch that disaster struck. One of the vans broke down altogether. To begin with we had hopes of it being a minor fault. We decanted everyone in a nearby country park for our picnic, while the remaining van was driven to the nearest garage for help. The mechanic who came soon disillusioned us. The repair would take several hours and the vehicle must be towed in to the garage. We decided that the only thing to do was to pile everyone and everything into one van and for Rosemary, Ted and me to proceed in that, leaving John and Margaret to come on when they could. The boys' excitement was in no way abated, but our spirits were considerably lower than when we had started. However, they lifted again as we approached the Welsh border and saw the hills, in sunshine, ahead of us.

We stopped at the border where there was an 'olde worlde' café. The boys wanted to stand on Welsh soil for the first time and, despite warnings, they spent money on a variety of 'gifts from Wales' probably made in Birmingham or Hong-Kong. From then on they asked every few miles, 'How much further?' 'Are we nearly there?' But as the road at length wound up on to bare hillsides, with mountains behind, they grew more silent. This country was bigger than anything they had seen before.

At last, we turned off the main road down a straggling village street and along a narrow road that followed the curves of a steep valley. The hills loomed high on either side, and we seemed to be driving right into them. We passed a few small stone farms, and then came in sight of about half a dozen cottages ahead. We drove slowly past. One cottage, with a bright flower garden in front, bore the notice 'Post Office'. A little further, a bow-windowed house displayed sweets, drinks and household goods. This was 'the' shop. Opposite stood a plain, well painted chapel, and beyond again the small Church of England. Then, the village was behind us. The road led over a stone bridge, and round a hill crowned with fir-trees. We turned a corner, and stopped at a gate on the left. Beyond it a track wound past the hill of firs and up to distant farm buildings. One of the boys opened the gate, and stood on the back as we bumped upwards towards the farm. As we neared it, there was a crescendo of barking and Mari came out of the house, waving. We had arrived at Bryn Uchaf.

The farm had belonged to John's family for many generations. As an only son he had inherited it, and he also looked after his aunt's farm further down the valley. A mile up the road, where it began to climb to the pass, was his sister's farm. But it was Bryn Uchaf which stood in the choice position, where a wooded side valley joined the main one and the mountains broadened out in a breath-taking view. From the old farm's front garden, meadows where John's Welsh black cattle browsed in summer sloped down to the tree lined river. The road by which we had come and the village were hidden behind the hill of the fir-trees, but looking straight ahead across the river one's eye travelled up and up the sallow grass slopes, studded with white specks as sheep grazed there, to mountain ridges high above. Away to the left, these ridges formed a great semi-circular barrier round the head of the valley. One could trace the ribbon of the road ascending it in a precipitous series of bends until it reached the top of the highest road pass in Wales and disappeared from view on its long and gentler slope down towards Bala Lake. When one turned and looked behind the farm, the hills were so steep that they hid the majestic summit of the Arran mountain towards which John's own mountain climbed steeply. But if one walked a few yards round the back of the farm, the side valley opened out, showing ahead high cliffs down which a waterfall tumbled, and beyond it the Arran's heights. On these hillsides a thousand or more of John's sheep grazed.

The new house stood in a prominent position, and its large windows framed the magnificent scenes outside. By contrast, the old granite and slate farm nestled into the hillside, its back kitchen literally scooped out from the earth behind. The windows in this house were small, built not for the view but with the idea of keeping out the cold. The house walls were two or more feet thick. A barn was built on to the house, and beyond it lay the old cow byre. The track leading up to the farm widened outside the buildings, and a small gate and wall separated it from the house's front garden. Down one side of the track a stream gurgled, and behind it stood the sheep dip. Some of our boys used to wash and clean their teeth in that spring water, preferring it to the large bowl of soapy warm water which we stood on a trestle table outside the house every morning. No breakfast without some attempt at a wash!

Little was changed inside the old house since I had first visited it, except that there was now electric light and a bathroom. The hub of the household was the farm kitchen. The parlour, on the other side of the front door and entrance passage, was formal and unlived in, dominated by a large and depressing painting of a lady on her death-bed. We used this room chiefly as a depository for children's belongings and for keeping outdoor games equipment. When it was wet, the boys' washing bowl was placed there. Our cooking was done in the back regions on a varied assortment of stoves. We lived in the main farm kitchen. Here a long refectory table stood below the window, with forms along either side. Another round table in the middle of the room was used as an overflow in the years we had to feed twenty or more. Along one wall a dresser housed games, books, paper and pens, and some cutlery. Inside the door hung a large-faced clock. This had a temperamental chime, and after one of Mari's more imaginative ghost stories, told in the firelight one night, it gained the reputation of being haunted.

The two features which dominated the room were the organ and the old grate with open fire and oak settle close beside it. The organ was something of an anxiety to us in case it got damaged, for boys were fascinated and would play, or rather make sounds, for hours on end until the rest of us could not bear the noise any more. As for the fire, we lit it when we got up and kept it going all day. One of the favourite chores was to chop wood from the pile that was always stacked outside the house. On wet days we strung lines across in front of the fire, and had to sit watching it through a curtain of dripping jeans and socks. Above the fireplace hung a Welsh text: *Duw cariad yar* (God is love), and if any household reflected that spirit, so that even the most unlikely youngsters felt something different, it was surely Bryn Uchaf.

That first visit however was anything but unclouded by troubles. In fact, looking back over the eight consecutive years in which we took camps to the farm, one of the most striking memories is of the change that took place among the boys who came that first year and returned with us so many times afterwards. Going back to that first visit, John and Margaret eventually arrived later on the first evening. The van was running, but not well, and we were thankful then that John Raynar had insisted that we should take the second. Throughout our visit we all travelled about in that. The boys, under

82

Ted's command, had got the tents up in the field crowned by the fir-trees, and had reluctantly dug the latrine according to Musette's instructions. We had brought Rosemary's own tent for Ted and John, and we women slept in low-ceilinged, dim bedrooms in the house.

One of my fears at least was not realised. I had been afraid that the boys would go off exploring at night, and might do damage. But they were all much too frightened of the dark. In London there was always a glow even in the darkest cul-de-sacs and, however badly lit, there was some light from the streets. This was their first experience of real darkness. When it was time for them to go down to their tents at night, they waited for one another and would not start until Ted led the way with his torch. Apparently it was the same when they wanted the latrine. No one would go on his own, without Ted. Even when they were all in their tents, with the flaps done up, they were still apprehensive and the sound of sheep cropping nearby or giving a cough sent them into a panic.

If they were afraid to get up and go out however, they were not afraid of making a noise themselves. Perhaps it was partly because they did feel afraid that they made such a din that first night, long after we had all tried to get them to be quiet. On subsequent visits we were prepared for a noisy and disturbed first night when everyone was over-excited and had been cooped up in a minibus for hours on end. But we also learnt to be patient. Strong fresh air and a lot of exercise soon began to tell. As the week wore on boys would invariably go to bed and straight to sleep. Another first night hazard that we learnt to expect was that after a very few hours of quiet, boys would wake in the dawn. Everything would look exciting and fresh outside, unless it was pouring with rain, and they would want to be up and doing. One year I was woken at a quarter to five in the morning by pebbles being thrown at my bedroom window. I opened it, and saw two boys ouside. 'What's wrong?' I asked, thinking one must be feeling ill.

'Nothin's wrong,' was the answer. 'Can we 'ave our spending money? . . .' (I kept it for them.) 'We want to go to the shop.'

Thinking back to the camps, the chronology becomes blurred, but incidents are indelibly etched against that lovely background. Gradually, too, traditions came into being: certain favourite things *had* to be done and places visited every year.

But that first year everything was new to us and there were times when we almost despaired. We still had to find out the best things to do and places to go. Besides, we ourselves had a lot to find out about the boys' reactions. We had not yet understood how traumatic an experience it was for them to be uprooted from their streets into such remote countryside, nor that it was largely an underlying fear of the unknown that sparked off their usual initial reaction of never wanting to do something new. The result was that we often set out on our expeditions exasperated and with the boys sulky and disgruntled, grumbling that they didn't want to go out, they wanted to lie in their tents, why shouldn't they, and so on. The first day when we suggested a walk we were met by fearful grumbles: 'Walk? Wot for? Why can't we go by van? Can't we stay here?' But it was not long before sulks were forgotten in the excitement of racing up hillsides, and by the time we had to turn and come home, the grumbles had changed to : 'Why can't we go on a bit? Must we go back?'

That is not to say that, when we were out, the boys saw what we saw. It was fun to them to leap from rock to rock over streams, to climb crags, to wrestle in the bracken, or to look for frogs. But of the wider views they saw little or nothing. We would point to some startlingly beautiful distant panorama, 'Look at that!' we'd exclaim. 'Wot?' they'd say, looking with sightless eyes. Some years later young John and his friends told us how they never knew what we were on about when we pointed to beautiful views until one day they were out on the hills alone (by that time we could let them go on their own) and suddenly the immensity of the hills, flowing in fold after fold to the horizon, struck them so forcibly that, they told us, they just stood and gazed and gazed. Though they had been up there often enough, they had never before looked at the view with *seeing* eyes.

It was difficult that first year to establish daily routines and chores. There was a struggle to get them up in the morning and there were continual moans, 'Let us alone'; 'We want a lie in'; 'Why should we get up?' After breakfast the group divided, and one section had potatoes to peel while the others washed up. We set a bowl and the potatoes on the trestles outside the front door and Ted's unenviable task was to round up fleeing figures and stand over them, while we supervised the washing up.

We still had a lot to learn about what supplies to take and what to buy locally. In future, we were to take all our food with us, except for fresh meat and some fruit and vegetables, as supermarket prices in Clapham Junction were much cheaper than foodstuffs in Dolgelley or Bala. The same applied to the stalls in the Battersea street markets, where in any case some of our boys worked and we could get produce at about half the price of the shops in Wales. One notable exception was our friend the butcher in Bala who sold us quantities of the best Welsh mutton for almost nothing because of his sympathy and unfailing interest in the camps.

We also had lessons to learn over the boys' feeding. That first year we tried to put theory into practice in giving wholesome meals with fresh meat and green vegetables. But at home some of the boys lived almost entirely on fry-ups, or pie and chips and fish and chips from the local shop. Beans were all right, so were fried onions, a few liked tinned peas but that was about it in the way of vegetables. As the week went by fresh air and exercise had their effect and appetites improved. Boys

85

who had begun by toying with cornflakes for breakfast were having two helpings of porridge before going on to eggs with fried potatoes and beans, and bread and jam. All the same, over the years we learnt to stick to well-tried menus for our main evening meal.

Most of the boys had hardly ever sat down to a meal with all their family together. Even at weekends in some cases, and always during the week, they were used to coming in when they felt like it and finding their food keeping hot in the oven or in a pan on the stove. They ate it standing at the stove, or perching wherever happened to suit them. The rest of the family did the same, so that there was no family dinner or tea-time, but just a succession of people eating as and when they pleased. To sit down all together was therefore a novelty, and to wait for grace to be said was sensational. Yet, strangely enough, the saying of grace soon came to be respected and indeed expected. In later years, if for some reason the adults were late in sitting down, one of the boys would, as a matter of course, say grace instead and no one would begin their meal until this was over. A ritual? Yes, in a way. But for some it went deeper than that and was linked with the opening out of a whole new concept of life itself.

On days when we were out, we took a picnic lunch with us, and we got used to arranging bread, butter and sandwich fillings precariously round us while we filled sandwiches and tried to keep up with outdoor appetites. When the food was finished we were left to wipe up crumbs, pickle smears and general mess. One year we had with us a helper who was a smart young air hostess, the daughter of family friends. When she got home she gazed at her once spotless trousers and told her mother she could recall each day's menu from the various coloured stains.

Another problem proved to be the relations between the boys themselves. At home they took one another for granted, but up here in a quite different environment boys showed very different and unexpected sides to their characters. This led to boys who had assumed that they were good mates, realising that they had not as much in common as they had thought. They began to go with different mates; there were feuds and the constant need on our part for diplomacy to smooth troubles over when it got to the stage of: 'If he's goin' – I'm not,' or vice-versa. There were also their arguments with poor Ted. These led to the famous 'Man Trap', especially designed for him. After one such row, the boys disappeared into the wooded gorge ostensibly to build a tree house. They had our permission and were busy for several hours. Under Tortoise's direction however their energies had not been entirely directed to the house. When Ted went out to find them later there was a tense silence as he got closer. Luckily he saw the hole in time, unskilfully covered by branches, and disappointed the watchers.

The morning that we left there was a nightmare pack-up and it was midday before we were ready to leave. John and Mari were there to say goodbye. John, fair-haired with very blue eyes and an open, kind face was much liked by the boys for he never talked down to them and always had a cheery word. By his side Mari was short, dark and, in spite of her efforts, plump. Her expressive face was as always on the point of breaking into laughter. She loved all young people and they felt it. Now she said goodbye to each one, and there was a warm hug for 'Johnny bach', who turned pink and tried to laugh it off though he was deeply pleased. It was probably the first time anyone had shown him spontaneous affection.

When at last we drove away, it was with mixed feelings. We were sad to leave the hills and friends, and we were still uncertain as to the success of the holiday. True, there had been good times when all had enjoyed themselves; the boys had glimpsed an altogether new world and people of another way of life; we had got to know them in a different way through living among them and had had several opportunities for discussing serious questions that had come up in the boys' minds.

We had also been spared illnesses and serious accidents, although young John had cut his head. On the other hand, there had been the moans and moods, and the arguments between the boys which had soured some of the time. We wondered what tales would circulate when we were all home again, and whether they would put others off coming away another time.

For most of that journey the boys slept like puppies sprawled along the seats. Once within sight and sound of London, however, they revived and grew more and more excited. When at last we drew up in front of the old chapel children came rushing at us from all directions, eager for news. From then on, throughout that autumn and winter, stories of wild adventures in Wales, told in vivid colours, were related and improved with the telling. All the grumbles and troubles were forgotten and groups of boys sat huddled round the old gas fire reminiscing for hours on end while others listened enviously. These tales had their repercussions, and the next year we took twenty youngsters to Bryn Uchaf.

That was the year of the red bus. We had not yet got transport of our own and we had been able to hire, for a minimal sum, an old coach belonging to the Mayflower Settlement in Canning Town. There was room in it for everyone, the luggage, and the tents and supplies and equipment. Moreover, roped along the roof was the canoe, now finished and ready for use. Our volunteeer driver did a noble job driving the heavy old bus which only just managed to grind up steep Welsh hills in bottom gear and had to have frequent rests to prevent boiling over. Unfortunately he was not used to boys from the sort of neighbourhood ours lived in and he so detested them, their language and their ways that long before we arrived in Wales the atmosphere was electric and it seemed uncertain whether, once we arrived, we would have a driver any longer. But relations did slightly improve, and games of cricket, which the driver was keen on, helped so that we were still able to use the bus on day expeditions.

We were exploring new places that year. We visited Dolgelley, grinding slowly over the pass on Cader Idris' shoulder, to the grey stone town on the beautiful Mawddwy estuary, reminding me of Cotman's distant view of it, all browns and blues. Every year after this, Dolgelley proved the favourite place for the youngsters to buy their presents. This ritual was new to me. As a child I had sent picture postcards home if I stayed away, and perhaps took some little memento home. But nothing like these children. Even those who had scarcely any spending money had to buy someting for every member of the family, however many brothers and sisters there might be, and they also included grandparents. Nothing would dissuade them from this.

We made a day expedition to the sea every year. In future years Harlech was to become a favourite place, and I have memories of several blistering hot days among the sand dunes there, with sand getting into all the sandwiches. Behind reared the dark walls and towers of the castle, and ahead miles of sand and blue sea curved round to the distant Lleyn Peninsula. Sometimes the sand was so hot that it hurt to go bare foot. The children would play in and out of the water, then hurry back to bury one another in sand, and, another popular pastime, to slide down the dunes. But in that second year all this was still in the future. Our visit to the seaside then was to a beach near Towyn. In those days one was allowed to drive along the straight road beyond the town to the river estuary which has since been taken over by the military. On this occasion, we had taken the canoe, which was joyfully unloaded on arrival at the river. One of our helpers was a canoeist and, donning life jackets, he and one boy launched the canoe. A queue of others waited their turn and we had a happy morning proving the workmanship of the canoe before carrying our picnic across the pebble ridge towards the beach. Several boys bathed, accompanied by Rosemary, but not all were keen to go right in the water. Some kept their jeans on and in all the years that Butch was with us he never got out of them at the sea, though before the end of the day he had always waded in to his waist. Then came the picnic, and afterwards most of us lay about, desultorily throwing stones. Presently I happened to stand up and look over the pebble ridge towards the road. I thought that I was seeing things. By some optical illusion the red bus appeared to move.

'Am I seeing things?' I called to the others and pointed.

'It *is* moving,' exclaimed Ted and began to run, thinking that the brakes must have been left off.

We all followed, and as we neared the road glimpsed Ernie's head through the side window. He saw us and ducked out of the opposite door amid shouts of laughter from the others. No harm was done, but after that no vehicle was ever left unlocked with ignition keys in it.

Another expedition that came to be a 'must' was our day at Bala Lake. We usually managed to pick a hot day. The little town, spoiled by selling itself to tourism, was crowded and after an hour or so for shopping in which we always visited our butcher friend, we were glad enough to leave the town and the main road, and to set out along the narrow old road skirting the far shore. There, several miles along, we had found the ideal picnic spot. We would drive the van across a farm track to a broad field, flanked by high trees, with the shore beyond. The boys fished, went in the canoe, swam, or lay in the sun. One year they made a raft, but we were wary of letting anyone far out, for this was a treacherous lake though very beautiful.

Nearer to the farm were expeditions along side-valleys, where there were deep rocky pools for swimming, and crags to climb. Several parties of boys, over the years, walked up the Arran with one of our helpers who had done some hill climbing, and returned in the evening, weary but triumphant. One day the lads were greatly intrigued by a worried man hurrying down to the farm to say that his female companion had had a fall and could not walk: could someone help? John was out, but full of enthusiasm, the boys sweated up the hill carrying an old gate. The woman had hurt her leg, and they put her on the gate and staggered down the hill with her. It was only as they reached the house that they realised they had carried her head first all down the steep slope. Mercifully, she was not badly injured and the boys' efforts had done no harm.

Another annual visit was to the Seven-Valleys hill top. We would never have found this had not Mari taken us the first time. It was a lovely evening of soft golden sun when she put her head in the window at the old farm where we had just had supper. She was in overalls after feeding the chickens. 'Why not come up to Seven-Valleys,' she said. There were cries of 'Yes! — Come on!' The boys loved Mari and were ready to go wherever she said. We dumped everything, piled into the van with Mari and me overflowing the front seat and Rosemary driving as usual. Down the valley we went, but with Mari accompanying us the drive was quite different. With her, every turn in the land assumed an identity of its own. That was the farm where the magic potion once killed all the livestock; here a witch had lived; there, the bandits of old had raided, climbing down the large chimney, and beyond lay the pool where the robbers had washed their blood-stained hands and the water was red to this day — 'Yes, Johnny-bach, to this day' — this to Butch, otherwise young John. Her musical voice lilted on. It did not matter that her English grammar was hopeless, or that she had to keep stopping to think of the English word, and not always succeeding. She transported the boys into another world, half fairy and ghost, redolent of sunshine, winds, hills, rain, everything natural.

It was no wonder that the journey down the lane was shorter than usual, and once through the village and on to the main road we nearly missed the side turn owing to the story telling. Certainly had Mari not been with us we should have missed it altogether. There was no signpost, and once in the lane no indication that it was ever going anywhere except on and on right into the hills. The lane climbed along a heavily wooded valley, and just went on. We passed only one cottage, and then on again. Finally we jolted to a halt as the road, now little better than a track, petered out in what had once been a farmyard but now looked deserted. Still no view. A narrow track led from the far side of the yard. This ended at a gate, and once through it the path, now only a sheep track, turned immediately and led through high steep slopes of bracken. Here we were in the open and could see where we were. The road had led us round the hills some nine or ten miles, but we had only to plunge straight down the bracken now to reach our own valley some two miles from the farm. We had not yet reached the crest of the long bracken slope. On we went, up a final grassy hill and then we were looking down on to Seven-Valleys, with mountains folding round them in blue masses, and far away to the south the long back of Plynlimmon visible against a glowing sky. The peace of those sunlit valleys, the golden glow of the hills fading slowly into deep blues and purples, the emptiness and the magic, enthralled us all. It was an infinity away from Battersea. But the spell cast by that view was short-lived. Those long, long slopes of bracken were too tempting. With a shout and a rush the younger boys were off, tumbling, chasing, rolling, bundling one another down to the bottom. Then up again gasping; then hiding, ready to fall out on the next boy to roll by. Bracken is a foliage which farms are only too eager to destroy, so no one was going to object to this glorious abandon, and when at last the boys were utterly exhausted, lying limp by the stream at the bottom, they looked with awe at the roads they had cut through the undergrowth, and which were plainly visible for the rest of our stay. While the boys were still flinging themselves up and down, we had set off for the van again. We drove slowly back down the long lane to the main road, and back through the village to our lane where we picked the boys up, limp, covered in dirt and bracken, but supremely content.

One occasion stands out vividly. John and Mari had the Head of a Bible College staying with them. He was kindly and anxious to make contact with our boys. One evening he came with us to the Seven-Valleys hill, and decided that he too would scramble down the steep hill. Knowing the boys' ideas of fun and their sort of horse-play, I took Les, now with long hair and a stubbly chin, aside and threatened terrible things if he did not look after our friend. He promised, and the great tumbling match began. Presently we sauntered on our way to the van. We had not gone far however before we heard a crashing of bracken and gasps coming up towards us. We stopped, and out of the high jungle appeared Les and Butch, pulling and pushing our friend, now speech-less and puce in the face. 'What on earth . . .?' I began.

'You said to look after 'im – so we thought you'd like 'im back up 'ere.'

The wretched man had got to the bottom safely, only to be hauled up to the very top! Whenever I have read his learned papers since I have thought of him that evening.

Our holidays always began on Saturday. On our first day at the farm we therefore had the problem of whether to go to church or hold our own meeting. John and Mari, like most of those who lived in the valley, were chapel-goers. There was no regular minister, but one came to hold a service on certain Sundays and on the others the people held a prayer meeting. However, all the meetings were of course in Welsh. We never found out what services, if any, were held in the church. Long ago the minister from Bala used to ride over the pass now and again to hold a service, and on Sundays the villagers posted a look-out. As soon as he saw the figure of the minister ride over the pass he would go to the church and ring the bell. By the time the minister arrived, his congregation would be waiting for him. The chapel-goers were helpful to us and, unless some special meeting had already been arranged, we took the youngsters there and the people held a meeting in English, usually with several people taking part and making the boys feel welcome. But the year of the red bus was a special occasion.

On arrival at the farm the previous day we had found that we were not the only visitors. Dr and Mrs Lloyd-Jones were staying with their old friends, Mari and John, in the new house. This was a delightful surprise for us adults who went to Westminster Chapel. All the same, I was not without some apprehension when I heard that the Doctor had agreed to take the chapel service the next day and would speak in English for our benefit. He admitted later that he had been tempted to refuse, but had accepted it as a challenge that as a preacher of the gospel he should be prepared to preach on any occasion, to any people, however seemingly impossible the situation. For the situation that Sunday was as difficult as any man could face. The tiny chapel, which scarcely held fifty people when full, would have half of its congregation made up of cockney lads who were ignorant of any form of church worship or religious conformity, the other half would be Welsh-speaking locals from a totally different background and culture who knew the Doctor as the greatest living Welsh preacher, drawing many hundreds from all parts of the Principality when it was known he was to preach – and here he was, unannounced, in their tiny chapel. Not surprisingly they were thrilled. As for the remaining few of us who regularly attended Westminster Chapel, we were used to being in a congregation of well over a thousand every week and to hearing the Doctor preach for an hour or more.

I was well aware that among some Christian circles in England there was an idea that the Doctor was a great intellectual who could only speak to those who were intellectually minded. I knew this indictment to be wholly untrue, as untrue in fact as to label John Wesley nothing but an Oxford academic. All the same I left it as late as I could before nervously shepherding our flock into the chapel that evening. The Welsh congregation was already there. The building had a central entrance door and I stood in it to direct our lot to the side that had been left for us. I had brought my large handbag with me since it held my reading glasses. But to the boys it represented my 'club bag'. Spontaneously, as they shuffled in, each delved into pockets or belts and produced a knife which he dropped into my bag. I glimpsed startled eyes of the congregation riveted upon us, and by the time the last boy had gone in my bag was spilling over with knives. I clanked in and sat as near the back as I could.

The boys' first astonishment as the service began was the volume and fervour of the singing that burst forth. After an uncertain giggle, they saw that many of the men of the valley were there and, like John, singing loudly. This was not a meeting for a few 'old dears', as they thought of church-goers at home, and it was not long before they were gruffly joining in, though without Welsh tunefulness. Wisely, the Doctor explained to the boys that he was going to speak in Welsh to the people for a minute, and after that the service would be in English. The boys sat still, fascinated by the strange sounds, as the Doctor thanked the Welsh people for sharing their service, and reminded them of where the boys came from. With good will established all round, the meeting continued.

There was spiritual power in the service that night. The Doctor took as his text the story of Paul preaching on Mars Hill, and explained in everyday terms the sort of people who listened to Paul, who their counterparts were today, what he had to say to them, and what it meant for us. There was not a long or complicated word or sentence in the whole sermon, and though the boys sprawled along the pews as they would anywhere else, they listened.

'That was good,' several remarked as they bunched out of the doorway afterwards. Two went further as they walked back to the farm beside me. ''E's all right, that bloke. I could understand wot 'e said,' declared one.

'Yeah – it's the first time I ever 'eard anything ter do with religion that made sense,' replied the other.

Another lad joined us and remarked: 'I could 'ear that bloke again. It were interestin' – 'E didn't talk down to us.'

Before Dr and Mrs Lloyd-Jones left Bryn Uchaf we all had a photo taken together. The boys did not forget him. Some time later an evangelistic team, without any local connections, held a mission near Clapham Junction and visited from house to house for a week in the area. One day I heard an altercation outside the chapel door. Several boys had been approached by the Mission leader and were being given leaflets and urged to attend meeings.

'We got our own,' I heard.

'But there isn't a minister here,' came the answer.

'We got our bloke,' they insisted.

'Who is that?' was the unbelieving query.

'Dr Lloyd-Jones. 'E's orl right.'

I came out to find total astonishment on the leader's face. He would have done better to think carefully about the implications for evangelism of what he had heard.

Two highlights of our annual visits to the farm were always our social evening with Mari and John in the new farmhouse, and the camp fire. The social evening had all the ingredients of a recipe for disaster, but was always a great success.

When we trailed over to the new house for our evening visit, Mari would open the door wide and welcome us in. For many this was the first social visit they had ever made, except to relations, and they were uncertain of themselves. Every chair in the house was brought into the parlour and the boys clumsily settled themselves, looking with interest at John's shotgun, hung far out of their reach, and at Mari's harp. One year one of the oldest lads wanted to buy the gun.

Usually Mari had also invited several girls from the valley for the evening, and it was interesting to observe people of two distinct cultures when they met. In the boys' eyes all girls were 'birds', to be chatted up, and they expected giggles and squeals in return. The only 'entertainment' they knew was the record player, the radio and the telly. But these girls, most of them from large families with several brothers, were not only capable of holding their own with the boys but were used, without self-consciousness, to making their own music and entertainment during a social evening. So were John and Mari; though John's glorious tenor voice was best heard when he thought he was alone in the cow byre or field.

The evening was usually divided into two parts, with a break for refreshments in the middle, when John could slip away to bed. Mari usually showed slides for part of the time. Invariably something was wrong with the projector and there were long pauses; and when it was working, the slides were in haphazard order and sometimes upside down. But it did not matter. In her broken English, Mari held her audience. They saw the farm under snow, with the mountains like Swiss scenes; the work of the farm through the seasons; Mari's old home, a big farm near Bala Lake; people no one knew, and as the years went by, most fascinating of all, pictures of themselves and of our groups. Then, when the projector was at last put away, Mari brought her harp forward. No one had seen one played before and everyone was interested as Mari or one of the girls performed, while the others sang. In this remote valley the difficult art of penillion singing was still current and to many of the boys, as indeed to us too, it seemed as the light faded from the hills outside and strange elongated shadows of the harp played over the walls, and the sound of unfamiliar singing and music rang out, that we had strayed into another world. In many ways we had. But the atmosphere changed and the fantasy was broken when Mari turned to the boys: 'Now – your turn! You sing for us, won't you?' It was natural for her to ask: wholly unnatural to them to be asked! But, after an initial embarrassed silence, the spell of the evening lured them on and they did their best. Untuneful as the Welsh girls had been tuneful, they gave us a succession of football songs.

Last of all, by popular request, Mari would tell stories. She would start hesitantly enough, but her vivid imagination soon took over and the most marvellous and ghostly stories of the old house and the valley followed, so that when at last we all departed into the dark the boys kept very close together. The evening however never ended with these stories, but with Mari singing an old Welsh hymn, accompanying herself on the harp, and finally with her telling some parable from the life of the farm. Those who heard never forgot the tale of 'Tim', John's best dog and how he learned to 'trust his master'; or the story of the sheep, marooned on a high ledge. The farmer hears its cry, but leaves it alone. Each day he returns, and hears the piteous cry, but only after several days, when the bleat is almost too feeble to hear, does he act. Then he gets ropes, and is let down the dangerous rock face to rescue his sheep and bring it safely home. While the sheep was strong enough to try to leap, the farmer dared not descend for fear it might jump to its death. So it is when we cease from our own strength, that the Good Shepherd receives us and leads us to safety.

Finally, Mari would look at the clock and remember that John must be up next morning. We all trooped back to the old house, after a unique evening without swearing, without suggestive or dirty jokes, without destructive horseplay, without 'pop' music, without 'birds' of the sort they knew, in fact without any of the things the boys in London regarded as a 'must'. Yet in months to come they would relive the evening over and over again. And the following year they would wait eagerly for the invitation. As they grew up too, they saw to it that the new youngsters who came for the first time

98

realised that this was something special. I remember one occasion when young John, now grown into a tall, bearded youth who was a trainee butcher, arrived at Mari's door ahead of the youngsters. As usual he had managed to hurt himself and was walking with the aid of a heavy stick. When the others reached the door he signed to them to file past him. He was a piratical figure, with stick raised and ferocious glare as he growled to each: 'You dare muck about – and I'll get you tonight. I ain't kidding.' There was no 'mucking about'.

The camp fire was held one night when the weather was good. It was built on the slope below the hill crowned with fir-trees, and with John's permission the boys spent many hours collecting dead branches and fallen tree trunks from the wooded gorge below. We waited until it was twilight before lighting the fire, and then it blazed in a beacon that could be seen far down the valley. We brought sausages and potatoes to cook in the embers, and the boys whittled pointed spears from sticks with which to hold the sausages. These were often charred before we got them, and the potatoes black on the outside but hard within, yet how good they tasted as we sat beneath the firs, with the scent of the trees mingling with wood smoke, and the sound of wind sighing in the branches above us! For a long time the boys rushed about, looking after the fire and poking potatoes. But gradually, as the flames began to die down, leaving a dull red glow, they threw themselves down nearby. Mari had come out to join us by then, and there was soon the demand: 'Tell us a story – a real creepy one.'

Mari is a born story-teller. Her English would sometimes fail, and she would exclaim: 'Now, tell me boys – what should I say?' And they would chime in. Then, in a lilting, dramatic voice she would go on. There was not a sound from the boys. The last light faded in the west; only the red glow of the fire lighted their eager faces.

And then Mari would stop: 'Now I'll tell you what's more real and more true than all that.' And she would tell them how she came to know the Lord Jesus Christ and how real he is, here and now. None of us ever pressed the boys to talk, but lying in the dying glow of the fire, they would talk and talk, asking us all sorts of questions about the Lord, and who he really is, and how we can really know him. At last, Mari would glance at her watch. Midnight. She would jump up, laughing. 'What am I doing here! Poor John will be asleep. You must be very quiet boys – he's up so early.' And off she would go, running. We would make sure that the fire was safe. The boys, already half asleep, would roll into their sleeping bags. As we walked up the track to the old house, we would stop and look back at the glow of the fire, the trees silhouetted black against the lighter sky, and the myriad brilliant stars. The only sound was the gurgling stream.

Those holidays were tiring, just at the time of year when most people are tired anyway, and the succession of helpers who came with us had to give up part of their own holidays to be free. But I believe that the weeks in Wales had lasting value for very many of the youngsters who were transported however briefly out of summer-stale city streets into a different world. After the first couple of years we had to take two parties each year for a week at a time in order to make room for those who had been before as well as newcomers, for younger boys and sometimes girls too. In varying ways and intensities they all did have their horizons enlarged and became aware of new ways of life.

One aspect of living which struck our urban young-sters forcibly, particulary those who came away with us most regularly, was the totally different attitude to work among the farmers they met, from anything they had known in the city. This is something we find still strikes lads today who meet other hill farmers. First, of course, their old ideas of farmers as straw-sucking ignoramuses had to be thrown out when they realised how many skills the small farmer has to have, and how self-reliant he must be, maintaining his own machinery as well as looking after livestock and land. Even more striking to our lads was the evident co-operation between men who helped one another without thought of payment, and, most revolutionary of all, the obvious fact that their work was an integral and satisfying part of life. It was not simply time grudgingly clocked off as hours spent to make money, in order that after work the business of living might begin. Here was a quite new concept of life and work to many urban youngsters.

In this and many other ways during the Welsh visits, curiosity was roused. Boys began to notice new things, question, and develop fresh interests. The proof of all this came after we returned to London when a number of youngsters continued with their new-found enthusiasms and their questioning attitudes. What was particularly striking over the years was that those who came away with us most regularly began to recognise these changing attitudes in themselves and to be able to speak of this. They began consciously to find that their old lethargic existences, punctuated by sporadic bouts of uncoordinated, destructive energy, were becoming boring, unsatisfying. They demanded new outlets of constructive activity, and opportunity to exercise initiative. Having tasted responsibility while away with us, some were prepared to take more on their return to London. In fact, these effects were so noticeable that they were, in due course, to become one of the strands in our thinking that led up to the 'Farm Project' which was to begin some years later.

As for the Christian basis of the camps, this was more difficult to explain to some of our zealous young student helpers who were used to the traditional children's summer camps, then run by various evangelical organisations. They found it hard at first to understand that while these last had a valid place among the children they catered for, from predominantly

101

church-going families, the very structured pattern on which they were run would be alien to our deprived youngsters from an inner-city area. What we were trying to do, however imperfectly, was to apply basic Christian principles without at the same time imposing an artificial code of behaviour on people who were largely ignorant of Christianity and of the types of up-bringing most Christians had known. In any case, I would not personally have felt it right to take those children away on what was for them a big adventure, and then to treat them as a captive audience for formal evangelistic meetings. The children all knew what we believed, and at Bryn Uchaf with John and Mari they experienced for the first time the love and warmth of a genuine Christian home. They felt this, and did not forget it. Back in London I was often told by mums of children who had been in Wales, that they 'wouldn't 'arf like ter meet them Jones' that the kids think so much of. They keep on about them. Lovely they must be.'

Apart from the formal Sunday meetings, we used to sit round the fire every evening after drinking cocoa, and we would tell them a Bible story or take up some Bible theme and try to bring out what meaning it could have for all of us in these days. They were not afraid of being got at and were therefore quite open in their questions and comments. This gave us the opportunity of finding out what they really thought, and whether they understood what we were telling them. One final but important point about the camps is that they were not one-off affairs where, after a week together, the children would go back home and we would never see them again. On the contrary, the interludes in Wales were an extension of the life centred round the old club in Battersea. There was no need for us to press youngsters to decisions, even if we had believed in doing so (which we emphatically did not), because the day after our return to London they would all be round to see us and to add a new season's reminiscences to their legends of Wales.

5: Sunday is a Different Day

'Go and look for the children,' I urged the earnest young man who had come to help with our children's Sunday-school and was standing while the rest of us rushed about getting ready for the afternoon classes.

'Where are they?' There was no sign of a child.

'Try outside the back door, on the roof, or down the cellar.'

The old building was not conducive to an orderly Sunday-school. Nor was the children's total lack of sense of time. In theory, three o'clock was when the meeting began. But some children straggled along soon after two oclock. They had nothing to do and nowhere to go. If we sent them away then the probability was that they would walk off and return again. So, while we prepared for the classes, we usually had children to contend with as well as constant thumps on the door from newcomers.

In order to cope with these staggered arrivals we began to prepare practical work – models, painting, and the like for the early-comers to do. But of course this necessitated freeing two helpers from our all too small number of adults to supervise. Without them the children soon found more exciting pastimes and areas to explore.

Before three o'clock, more helpers would go out to collect various 'regulars' from their flats. Often they would be gone a long time. The children had only just begun dinner, or were not even dressed. In homes where Dad went to the pub, dinner would not be ready until after three and the children had to come to us without having eaten, when they came at all.

The very small nucleus remaining from the 'nice little children' we had started with, arrived at the proper time having been sent by their mothers. But these were greatly outnumbered by the more boisterous contingent, which was not surprising. The building itself was not a 'nice' modern place, and in our weekly visiting, we found that the more snobbish among the mums were not enthusiastic when they heard that we came from the derelict old building where so many noisy 'kids from the streets' went. To many of them, churches and Sunday-schools were for respectable folk – and *no one else*. Indeed, one man told me: 'There was a time when no one but respectable, well-dressed people would go in there,' and he pointed to the chapel. I wondered whether that was why the place had virtually died. It was my first experience of what has become one of our most serious problems ever since: that of integrating different types, social classes and, latterly, different colours. This has been far more marked since the old houses disappeared and the modern blocks have taken their place. But hints of this already existed even in our first years. Nothing brought this out more clearly than the advent of the 'Durham Buildings' children.

To begin with, we had not known the existence of such a place, but my curiosity was roused by constant references to it. Whenever anyone appeared looking particularly bedraggled, after tearing or otherwise ruining his clothes, someone would invariably taunt him with: 'Where'd you get them things – Durham Buildings?' Or, if a kid wanted to be particularly insulting he would jeer: 'Moved inter Durham Buildings, ain't yer?' And everyone would laugh.

'What and where is this Durham Buildings?' I enquired.

'Can't yer smell it?' was the immediate response. Further enquiries brought to light that it was a block of buildings, originally artisan dwellings but for some time used by the Council for accommodating problem families who for one reason or another had gone down and down the housing scale until they had reached this 'low'. They could descend no lower than Durham Buildings. I never saw the famous TV programme *Cathy Come Home*, but nothing in that can have been more horrendous than conditions there.

The Buildings consisted of a number of five-storey blocks, joined together in a forbidding row, and facing onto a busy main road where heavy vehicles thundered past by day and night. In order to reach the entrances to the various blocks one had to go through a gloomy archway which led to a narrow concrete yard, bounded by a high brick wall. Behind this reared the ugly buildings of Gartons Glucose Works whose high chimneys belched out the distinctive and unpleasant 'Battersea Smell'. Stone staircases led up through the blocks and from these came an evil stench. The latrines opened onto the stone landings of the stairways. They were communal to the flat dwellers, and presumably no one had responsibility for cleaning them. Usually a thin stream of urine trickled from under the door and down the stairs, making sodden the filth that littered the steps and joining with stale vomit from the previous week-end's drunkenness, to make a literally nauseating stench. In the summer flies buzzed around unhealthily.

The first time that I stepped through the dim archway and came out into that awful yard, I felt as if I had stepped back a century into Dickens' London. Rosemary was with me, and as we stood and stared, appalled, at the dirt and sheer ugliness, a mob of ragged, dirty looking children rushed at us. We disentangled ourselves with difficulty from clutching arms and hands, and moved determinedly to the stairs of the first block. Several women who had been sitting on the steps stopped gossiping and stared, but we edged past them. We had decided to go to the top and work our way down, calling at each flat to make contact with mums, telling them who we were and why we would like to take their children to Sunday-school. With most, we need not have bothered to explain ourselves: anyone who would take children off their hands for an hour was more than welcome.

We went on visiting week by week until we had been to every flat and had talked with all the extraordinary assembly of human flotsam who lived there.

There was a dragon of a woman in the office whom years of experience had left embittered and hardened. 'Don't bother about them,' was her advice. 'They'll take all they can, and you'll get no thanks, only abuse and trouble. They can all tell a marvellous tale – don't listen. It's not worth it.' I retorted that we had not come looking for thanks. They were human beings, the same as us. She evidently doubted this, and we parted on mutually bad terms. In future I did my best to avoid 'the dragon'; but sometimes I could understand her viewpoint.

People existed in Durham Buildings for all sorts of reasons. Undoubtedly there were some who deliberately made themselves homeless by various devices, such as getting parents to turn them out, by choosing to default on the rent, and by other means. Their reason was that once they were at Durham Buildings they were likely to be rehoused in a good new flat much more quickly than if their names were still near the bottom of the housing lists in the borough. But these only represented a small percentage of the inmates of the Buildings. There were women whose husbands had left them, and who could not cope with providing for a family on their own; there were single women with illegitimate children, sometimes four or five of them. There were those whose husbands were in prison and who had lost their previous accommodation for that reason. There were immigrants, at that time not nearly so many as there would be today. There were couples, in which the man was an invalid and the wife incapable of coping; and there were the borderline mental cases. In fact, you name the domestic problem, and it could have been found in that stinking, degrading building.

An Irish family was among the more colourful and

attractive of these families whom we got to know. There were eleven children. Father hardly ever appeared; mother was invariably clad either in a negligée and curlers or in what seemed to be full evening dress. I never discovered just what her 'work' was, nor why the family was in Durham Buildings, since there never seemed to be any particular shortage of money, and when we had outings, the children all had sufficient pocket money. Besides, in spite of the surroundings, they were basically a happy family unit. The younger ones whom we got to know well were headed by Janet, who looked after the youngest of the brood like a mother, though herself only eleven. We took her on holiday one year, and as so often, a week of actively living with children tells you more about them than years of more remote contact. Janet had one of the pleasantest dispositions of any girl we have known, genuinely unselfish and helpful, but ready to join in fun with the others, so that everyone liked her in spite of the 'Durham Buildings' label. Her chief charge at home was the next in age, Mary, a spastic child with constantly dribbling mouth and jerking limbs that sometimes had a violent sudden pain making the child scream fearfully. Mary was gentle and affectionate and any treats or outings gave her immense pleasure. The little boys were likeable ruffians, full of noise but not surprisingly on the defensive with others as the brand of Durham Buildings was upon them, condemning them from the beginning. This family came to us regularly for two or three years, and Janet at least integrated with others better than the rest. Then they moved to a house in another area where they still live, and are securely rooted in society again with the old stigma largely forgotten.

Not so another large young family whom we knew well in those early days. Father was sometimes a self-employed decorator, quite when I have never known. Now and again, they would appear in great excitement, saying they were all going to be rich 'next week' when faher was paid for his last job. But somehow 'next week' never came and nor did the money. Their flat was certainly no recommendation for his business, with wallpaper stripped off ready for redecorating that was never done. The mother used to tell me she came from a gipsy family and could not read. She was unhealthily possessive with her children, half smothering them and isolating them from any hope of making relationships with other children. The clan indeed was a by-word, even among other children at Durham Buildings, and the unfortunates took the only refuge open to them of withdrawing into themselves and a fantasy world. For a long time they came to us, and when alone were responsive, but as soon as they had to mix with others, the protective shutter came down isolating them not only from the harshness of insults and degradations, but from human society in general. The last I heard of them was that they had moved on to another equivalent, though less degrading, of Durham Buildings.

One family, of indeterminate national origin, I remember had no furniture in their flat except a bed and a television set, and in the kitchen a table. The two or three little children would sit cross-legged in front of the telly, while father and mother sat or lay on the bed. But that state of affairs came to an end when the mother threw herself out of the window and was killed. Tragedies, ambulances, Authorities and Police were the ordinary pattern of living at Durham Buildings, and of course news of each latest event spread like a bush fire. The atmosphere was crude, sometimes violent with fights, not just between youngsters but with men, and even women, whose tongues in any case could be vicious as they sat on the stone steps leading on to the concrete. Yet in the midst of all this, we used occasionally to come across an immaculate doorstep, and on ringing a polished bell would be ushered into a spick and span flat, with children cared for and the mother concerned about them. In similar circumstances I doubt whether I, or the majority of 'well-to-do' women I know, would have coped nearly as well as those few I was privileged to meet at Durham Buildings.

Nearly everyone was prepared to talk to us, to listen to what we had to say of the Christian Gospel and the hope it held out for all, no matter what our situation, if we would only turn to it. Some women came to our Women's Meetings, though chiefly because it represented an afternoon out with tea and biscuits. And who could blame them for wanting a brief escape? On Sunday afternoons we brought the minibus which my mother had by then acquired for us, outside the Buildings and as soon as the lookouts reported that we had arrived, there was a stampede and we returned with a load of screaming, kicking and often smelling children.

When we began bringing these children I had naively not anticipated the reaction among our regulars at the club. After all, many of them came from rough homes, and calamity might even land them in the Buildings too. Certainly it was not the *children*'s fault that they were condemned to such sub-human surroundings. But that is not how our members saw things.

'Ugh! Durham Buildings!' they exclaimed in disgust, and refused even to sit near the newcomers.

'My mum says they deserve all they get.'

'My dad says, Why should we be taxed to support layabouts like them.'

'We don't want 'em 'ere.' This last was the unanimous cry.

All the same we continued to bring them. I believed that it was important to try to show by example the Christian principle (as opposed to the Pharisaic one) that our Lord himself moved among the outcasts, many of whom were probably extremely evil-smelling and foul in personal habits; and that his gospel is not for the self-righteous but for those who acknowledge their failure and seek him, whoever they are. But my attempts to explain that there was no Christian justification for refusing those who were down and out, even if parents had brought troubles on themselves, largely fell on deaf ears, as did my strictures that none of us were perfect: which of us should throw the first stone? Prejudice was terrifyingly strong. It was a long time before barriers were broken down, and then only among a few. Other youngsters remained a colony apart.

Ever since the departure of the City missioner and the intrusion of the first boys, we had been struggling to think out what basic principles should under-gird how we ran the Sunday-school, and how these should be applied. It had taken no time at all to realise that conventional Sunday-school methods were hopelessly inappropriate. That was when we lost our replacement leader and were left to manage on our own. It was much more difficult to work out the right way forward with such a mixed multitude, especially as we had to do so in and through a living situation, rather than being able to sit quietly in an armchair and theorise. It did not help that at that time in the sixties there were a number of 'armchair Puritans' about (those who read Puritan works but were not activated as the genuine Puritans had been by intense concern for others) to whom everything appeared simple, who in any case did not think much of Sunday-schools and still less of women. As always, however, we could count on the encouragement and wisdom of Dr Lloyd-Jones who urged us to take no notice of what others said, but to get on and do our own thing in the way we were led to do it. That, by and large, is what we did.

We were considerably helped when Brenda Mason came to teach the little ones. She was then Assistant Headmistress at a Junior School near Waterloo and, besides being a concerned Christian, she had the practical experience which we lacked, in communicating with young children from tough city areas. I can see her now in our dreary back room, sitting among nearly twenty lively children, yet somehow holding their interest.

The rest of us learned slowly and painfully over the

months that there were two basic considerations which we must not neglect. We had, on the negative side, to deal with and answer popular misconceptions, or else there would be continual confusion. This was true even among tiny children. In spite of (and in some cases because of) RE lessons, primary and junior school children were often already muddled between fairy stories and Bible stories. Their school Christmas pageants brought in fairies and nymphs as well as angels, and they knew more about Mary's donkey than about who her son was. At home, their little minds were further confused by TV and to add to their troubles, their sharp ears and eyes soon took in that mums and dads thought that it was kids' stuff anyway and nothing to do with 'real life'. So, not surprisingly, as the children left babyhood behind they wanted to rid themselves of 'baby' ideas. Out went all the fairy stories from their thinking, and with these went their muddled Bible stories. In their place they accepted without question whatever popular fallacies happened to be trendy at the time, and adopted like parrots the age-old clichés and catch questions as if they were new:

'How can I believe in God unless I can see him?'

'My mum says – there can't be a God, or he wouldn't let there be mongol kids or spastics.'

'What's your God doing about . . .?' Any number of things came in here from bombs and starving people to an old woman losing her purse.

'Why should we believe the Bible? It's only a book.'

'On telly it said Jesus was only a man, or he didn't exist, or he couldn't save himself, let alone anyone else.' And so on and so forth. Until we had cleared this clutter away we could not build up their understandings.

On the positive side, the second step we had to take was to examine ourselves, to make sure that we had thoroughly digested the fundamentals of what we believed, and that we could communicate simply, in words that the children would understand. Most of us soon learnt that it was all too easy to imagine that we were conveying some thought, when in fact the children understood something different from what we said, or understood nothing at all. It was no good assuming background knowledge, nor understanding of 'religious' words. For instance, how many hymns and choruses use the word 'holy', and how easy for us to use it without explanation in telling a Bible story or speaking about God. But it meant nothing to our hearers, unless they thought of tattered and torn clothing. Then there were words like 'Father' and 'love'. Again, how many hymns and choruses use these; and how often Christians speak of God as 'our Father', and pray in those terms assuming that their hearers can follow their meaning. But how much the word needed to be explained to our young hearers, whose concept of father was enough to put them off any being described in those terms! For many the word was associated with unreliability and hasty temper, drunkenness, beatings, and occasional over-indulgence. What a way to think of God, our Father! Likewise the word 'love' was so debased in their understanding that it meant nothing but lust or sex; and to talk of the 'love' of God was to give them a blasphemous concept. The word 'sin' had no meaning for them, and 'saint' either conjured up pictures of stained glass windows and figures with halos or of Simon Templar alias 'the Saint'. 'The Devil' was just a make-believe, somewhat comical figure with a toasting fork in his hand; 'angels' were fairies; 'hell' was good for a laugh; 'heaven' was dull and dreary; and 'hallowed' held no meaning at all.

Those were words which many of them had heard before, but which were devalued in their meaning. But there were others which Christians use glibly, and which were double-Dutch to our hearers: words such as redemption, resurrection, atonement and communion, to say nothing of terms like justification or sanctification. But even when difficult words were avoided, one still had to guard against giving complicated descriptions and using thought-forms which were outside their range. They were not used to conceptual thinking, but to straightforward, plain speaking. At home they grew up with short, sharp remarks, without any of the descriptive padding or gently phrased suggestions most of us were brought up with. They hardly read at all, and their vocabularies were strictly limited. All this meant therefore that if we were concerned for the children, rather than to air our own knowledge like the speaker at our Women's Meeting who addressed them on the cosmic fall, we could not repeat phrases like parrots, but had to put ourselves under very strict discipline and ask ourselves just why we were saying this or doing that. If we did not, someone else inevitably would.

We held our Sunday-school in the afternoons, chiefly in order that we might go to church ourselves in the mornings. We had a quick lunch, and everyone arrived at our old building as early as possible. When most children had arrived, we all assembled in the main hall where we prayed and sang one hymn or chorus to the accompaniment of a battered piano, played by a magnificent old lady who looked severe, with hair scraped back into a bun and hat stuck firmly on her head with large hatpins, but who had a heart of gold. The little ones would sing and act out their choruses when they retreated into the back 'kitchen' for their class, but the rest of us had no more singing. This was because, contrary to what I was told by teachers in Sunday-schools where the children came from a different background, our older children hated singing, particularly the boys. We could not see the point of forcing it on them, and decided that it was more important to teach them what Christianity is about and then they would have something to sing about.

I used to give out news of any special events, and then would attempt one short general lesson that was part of a weekly series, before we split up into different age groups for the rest of the afternoon. I found that the sort of trendy stories I sometimes read in children's Christian magazines and Sunday-school aids, in which modern children featured and illustrated a biblical parallel or moral, were not appropriate. They were usually associated with a different type of child and background, and our children failed to see the point of the story, and dismissed the characters as snobs or drips. Having learnt that, I seldom deviated from straightforward Bible stories, illustrating doctrine and application through these. No-one ever found these characters 'drips'. No matter how wide the age group or how mixed the children's backgrounds, the stories spoke directly to them, as one should expect if they were from the Word of God and not from our imagination. One classic exception, I was to find, was *Pilgrim's Progress*, whose story and characters also had an immediate impact.

We began to make up our own teaching syllabus and in our teaching we included a text to learn. This sounds old-hat to some these days, but they should take note that the advertising media have understood only too well the importance of implanting a slogan into a child's mind. It seems to me that in these days when a child is confronted at every turn with materialistic suggestions and slogans, it is if anything even more important that while their minds are in the most receptive, formative state, they should be helped to lay a foundation of basic Scriptures, provided of course that they are taught what these mean. They will be a bulwark against ideas that harm and destroy; they can help to form sound judgements; and how often do we hear of texts being remembered in later years and at crucial times!

Our teaching syllabus included making sure that any words we read or sang were understood. 'What does salvation mean?' I asked one day, when it had come up in the singing. Dave's hand went up. 'It means yer very hungry,' he shouted. We also had to teach children how to find their way about the Bible, since it was literally a closed book to them; and, most important, in our general lesson, I had to teach them what the petitions of the Lord's Prayer meant, when we repeated them

Sunday after Sunday. Another series which we taught to each new generation, was the Ten Commandments. If anything, the importance of teaching these has assumed greater importance in my mind over the years, and we make certain that all our youngsters both learn them and discuss them thoroughly. It is such a novelty to most children of pagan Britain, that they look forward to what's coming next, sometimes urging one another: 'Come on, it's *Commandment* time.'

The particular importance of teaching our children from the Commandments seems to me that they reveal so much about God himself as well as about how his world should be ordered and how we should live in order to function fully and properly. After all, there is little point in telling children about Jesus Christ and why he came to live in the world if they have no idea who God is, of his character, or his basic laws for the world and for us. Without a glimpse of God's holiness, how would we or they ever begin to see our inadequacy and failure to meet his mark, or to understand our need of the Lord Jesus. To most of our children the name God was simply a popular swear-word, and we therefore had as a first priority to introduce them to the character of the person who takes the trouble to tell us so much about himself in the Bible as well as in the world around us and in the make up of our own human personalities. Unless we started with God himself, which is where the Bible starts, it seemed to us that the gospel itself would be virtually meaningless. But each Commandment could be illustrated by a host of Bible stories, and each in its way pointed to our need for forgiveness and power to live a new life, in fact to our need of salvation through Jesus Christ.

It was not a question, however, of nice little children sitting patiently to listen to us. I was often thankful for a loud voice that could roar over background noises and shrill interjections. In our individual classes children spent some time in handwork and activity relating to whatever we were talking about and learnt as much that way as if they had been sitting still. In fact, in years to come I was often surprised by older boys and girls reminding me of some lesson that I thought no one had listened to at the time.

At tea-time on Sundays when the young children clattered out, older teenagers arrived whom we did not want to insult by including them with the 'babies'. These sessions were even more informal. They sat or sprawled on chairs, tables, the floor or window sills, drinking their tea and listening (or not) to what we had to tell them. After that, we were open to discussion and to various handicrafts. For instance, during one autumn they painted a series of pictures about how the Bible had come down to us in England. During another period, they wrote out and painted in enormous lettering the Ten Commandments. When they were completed we put them up all round the top of the walls. There they stayed for all to see and proved a great means of attracting attention and starting discussion in our weekday clubs.

Inevitably questions used to come up as to why we made a difference between Sunday and any other day, and why our weekday activities such as snooker and table-tennis were put away. It was not hard to explain our reasons. What was more difficult was to answer questions as to why certain churches and professing Christians play their football teams in Sunday Leagues or hold public sports and discos on Sunday evenings, and so on. We were also up against the glib idea that Sunday is a day of rest (ie to stay in bed till dinner time, if you like), but not to rest from anything you may feel like, or to rest *from* ordinary daily activities in order to give the day *to* another purpose. That was altogether a new idea to them. But what stuck out a mile to us was that their Sundays, 'liberated' from any significance and purpose, bored them to distraction.

The highlights of the Sunday-school year, if you were one of the children, were our annual summer outings, the Chrismas party and the Christmas family afternoon with pageant. For some weeks before the first and second event the Sunday-school swelled noticeably with the punctual arrival of even the most erratic attenders. As for the third, in time we learnt wisdom (or cunning?) and arranged to hold the family afternoon before the weekend of the party. We wanted as many as possible to be there to hear the message of Christmas.

The summer outings had a Joyce Grenfell flavour to them. For us helpers, they began the evening before when we had to prepare, make and collect sandwiches, dozens of cakes and biscuits from volunteer cooks. The children brought their own packed lunches, most of which were eaten before we had left the outskirts of London, but we gave them tea and ices before the journey home. Weather of course was all important, and if we woke to leaden skies on the morning of the great day our spirits drooped accordingly. The coaches were due at about nine thirty am. for a long journey or ten o'clock for a shorter one, but by half past eight a few children had always gathered outside. I had a list of names, and each child had to be ticked off and his money collected, usually only a few shillings in the early years, before he was allowed inside the building. Once in they could not go out again, and there was a rising tide of excitement and noise. By the time that the coaches drove up, some of the youngsters had already lost their sandwiches or their swimming things. I always had to send a few home, if there was time, to get a jersey (this was stipulated on their form and forgotten) or to change out of high-heeled shoes. Always, too, several families were missing. Messengers were despatched at a run, while we attempted to quell the rush of children to the buses and bring about some sort of order as they climbed on board. In the background the drivers looked on, some very tolerant, others already glum and glowering. We had to wait for the return of our messengers, with or without the missing children, though usually with them: 'Our mum never woke up,' or 'we didn't know the time.' And then, exhausted before we had begun, we were off. It would not be long before the paper bags of food came out, and the children would be asking: 'Are we nearly there?'

It was a problem to know where to go each year. Tradition said, to the seaside. But after several years of conforming we varied it and set out for pastures new. Going to the coast had several drawbacks. First there was the long, slow journey down crowded summer roads, when one or two children were bound to be sick on the way there and several more, having stuffed themselves, on the way back. The long journey also meant less time actually at the beach, and in fact coach-drivers were in a perpetual hurry to get us all loaded and away again. Then there was the seaside itself.

We wanted to avoid places with too many amusement arcades as we knew that the children would disappear into them rather than enjoy fresh air and sunshine. We did not want to go where a busy road lay between the shore and the lure of sweet-shops and ice-cream stalls. Lastly, there was the problem of finding the right sort of shore. Little ones obviously liked sand; bigger ones wanted rock pools and other excitements to explore; we wanted safe bathing and not too many crowds. It was virtually impossible to find the ideal, at least within reasonable distance, and the more suitable the environment, the greater the number of other Sunday-school outings and excursions there were likely to be. This was particularly true of Littlehampton. We went there several times in spite of the distance, because of the lovely sands, but gave it up after one occasion when in hot sunshine it seemed as if every other Sunday-school in the South of England had also chosen to go there. The tide was out, leaving an enormous expanse of sand. Children set out to bathe in parties accompanied by an adult, but inevitably some began to straggle back on their own, while others wandered off collecting shells and stones and then could not find us again for all the other thousands of groups. A number of more efficiently organised parties than ours had large flags or banners erected on poles, bearing the name of their group. That was the day when Mrs Jenkins, one of our most valued helpers and wife of the General Secretary of the EMF (European Missionary Fellowship), had to be stationed permanently in the Lost Children's beach hut.

The first year that we broke with tradition and went into the country instead of the seaside we were blessed with a hot sunny day. We went to a delightful spot in the Surrey hills near where Mr Fred Pride was then involved in the work of a tiny chapel. It was he who told us of the place, a natural grassy glade surrounded by woods, with paths through them to explore and, best of all for our boys, high sand hills to slide down. There was a safe lane, leading in two hundred yards or so to the mecca of a village shop well stocked with sweets. Everyone, even the coach-drivers who departed for the pub, was content. There was room for cricket for the more organised, for little ones' games, and for marvellous exploring parties. 'Sardines' was popular, and I managed to be so well hidden that I had a pleasant sleep before returning to the fray.

The hot sunshine largely made the success of that day. Not so on our visit to Frensham Ponds! I had taken the precaution of booking the village hall for the afternoon 'just in case', and my worst fears were realised. Grey clouds and drizzle accompanied us on the journey, but once we were out of the coaches and straggling round uninviting stretches of choppy grey water, the heavens opened. The downpour continued without a break all day, and we had to play games, also without a break, until we thankfully gave the children tea and climbed into our coaches. I had hardly seen the well-known beauty spot, but that day put me off for ever!

Two of our more popular excursions which we were to repeat several times, were to Knebworth Park and to Ruislip Lido. We took the Sunday-school to Knebworth the first year that it opened as a country park and though some of its later attractions had not yet been added there was an exciting adventure playground. In addition, everyone there was keen to send us away happy in order to publicise the place, so we had special pony-rides and even a display by a Police-dog and handler. In later years it became much more expensive to go there, but the great advantage of the place was that there was plenty for all ages to do. Even the mums who came could, if they wished, take a tour of the house, go and sit in a café or explore the gifts and garden shops.

It was at Knebworth one year that we got as near as we ever did to losing a child. This was Josie, then a bright-eyed, rosy-cheeked and quite fearless little girl. Back on the coaches, we always had a final count before starting home. This was not quite as simple as it sounds; it took time to be sure who in fact was missing. A search party returned to the adventure playground. No Josie was to be seen. The party fanned out in all directions, Still no Josie. We began all over again back at the adventure playground. We had just drawn a blank, when someone happened to glance up, no longer looking for Josie, towards tree tops nearby. She looked again more closely, then shrieked. Josie was perched on one of the top branches, gently crooning to herself, enveloped in a leafy world of her own and watching the birds.

The attraction of Ruislip Lido was, again, that there was something for everyone. Added to that, it was a comparatively short journey to get there, and in those days it was cheap. There was an enclosed mock beach for little ones, bordering on a shallow stretch of lake, well wired-in for their safety, where they were just as happy as at the seaside. There was a miniature railway through the woods; there were places for fishing; and farther round the lake were swimming areas for older children and adults, lawns for sun-bathing and games, and kiosks selling sweets and ices. Besides all that, there were usually water-skiers out on the lake to watch. Best of all from our point of view, the whole was fenced-in like a prison. Apart from a few cuts and bruises those

120

days were without serious incident, though I recall poor Mrs Jenkins, ever willing, stepping backwards and falling into deep water. Another time there was a sudden torrential thunderstorm, almost tropical in its intensity, which drenched everyone.

As a further variation on these outings, we sometimes took the oldest class of boys and girls by minibus on a special longer day's excursion, such as to Beaulieu Motor Museum and the New Forest, while the younger ones had their coach trip to one of the usual places. But whatever the destination, the one constant factor was our own exhaustion when we drew up at the club and were met by various parents and older brothers and sisters. With difficulty we got rid of the last children, and staggered in to the club with our bats, balls, ropes, empty cake tins, and containers of orange drinks. Even then our day was not yet over! Everything had to be put away, and the place prepared for Sunday-school next day.

At least the Christmas party lasted for only three hours. But what hectic hours they were! Besides, we had always spent the evening before and the whole morning of the day decorating the hall and preparing food. Some of the boys helped with decorating, and were skilful in hanging paper chains and bells. The only trouble was that, left to themselves, they would begin decorating one another and binding someone in miles of streamers or playing basketball with the paper bells. The tree also had to be decorated, not too lavishly or the various ornaments would be 'nicked', and it must not stand where children could too easily finger it. No one but adult helpers and some of the girls were allowed in to prepare and put out plates of food. Jim's special task was to erect an adventure course in the old chapel. He helped us for years and was wonderfully ingenious in improvisation, but the various contraptions made from ladders, beams, forms, mats and ropes rearing out of pews and suspended from the balcony were hardly ever finished before the party began and children swarmed in and made a bee-line for them. In a few minutes tidy clothes were covered in dust and frilly dresses had taken on a Cinderella-in-the-ashes look.

Once more I had to be ruthless over who was admitted – Sunday-school ONLY. The trouble was that we had no room for anyone else. As might be expected, the Durham Buildings contingent were always there in force, as they were for the outings. The old building was not in the least suited to these parties. Everyone had to come into the main hall, where we wanted to set out the tea, and then be forcibly pushed away from temptation through to the chapel area for games, and somehow be kept from straying back or from tearing one another to pieces, for an hour. Relentlessly we locked the door on them all, only answering urgent knocks when someone had to go to the toilet. Then that little person had to be escorted past all the cakes and crackers and jellies to the grim outside toilet, and back again. Meanwhile at least four different games and activities had to go on in the chapel simultaneously to cater for the age groups, and even then there were those who could not relate to others, but who drifted round the edge.

When tea was ready I blew a football whistle, keeping the door closed behind me. It took a long time and many threats before we got the smallest children safely through the scrum to the front and let them in to the tea tables to get settled. Afterwards in a seething, erupting, two-by-two crocodile, the children writhed in and clambered on to chairs. Crackers had already been removed from reach, and balloons hung in bunches near the ceiling. At last everyone was sitting, and after shouting over the tumult, I had a semblance of quiet for our Grace. Then it was a free for all. Some children ate nicely taking one thing at a time; some were like squirrels collecting a winter's supply beside them; others licked or bit one cake, then went on to another. But at least for ten minutes or so there was blessed silence. Jellies followed the cakes – then crackers, and with them peace was shattered with a blast of whistles, rattles, shrieks and loud bangs.

Since we had to shift everything to prepare for the next 'scene', all the children were herded back into the chapel for more games, though with less enthusiasm now. A treasure-hunt went some way towards restoring this. Meanwhile we rushed round outside, clearing the debris, sweeping, and setting out chairs in rows while someone got the projector and screen ready. As soon as we could, we gave the helpers in the chapel a reprieve. Everyone poured back and sat down; lights went off and catcalls resounded, until the first of the cartoons began. Then there was immediate silence, and no matter how feeble the films were, there was continued attention. But at last the show was over. I prepared the audience for a visitor. There had to be quiet – and there was throbbing expectant silence. Into this, came three loud knocks. I opened the door. Father Christmas with weighty sack, was on the threshold.

Everyone had to come up for his or her present, each of which was labelled by name. This took a long time, and as soon as the last present was given, our pianist struck up as loud as possible with a carol everyone knew. By then, parents had begun to arrive to collect children; and as the music died away, some older boys who had come to help Jim, were ready on ladder tops to let the balloons down. That was the end, except for the scrum round the balloons, and round the coats for we had no cloakroom or even hallway. It was dark and we did not like young children going home alone, so while some piled into the van, others were escorted on their way on foot. Inside the hall any remaining cakes were greedily gobbled by older youths and girls from the clubs, and we adults settled for strong tea before, once again, the sweeping up and cleaning began to transform the place for Sunday-school next day.

The Christmas pageant had quite a different purpose from the other two 'treats' for our children. It took place at least a fortnight before Christmas, not simply because we wanted to hold it before the party, but because we wished as many children and parents as possible to hear the reason for celebrating Christmas, in time to offset some of the massive publicity campaigns designed to denigrate the festival to food, parties, booze, a spending spree, and presents. These were the strident advertisements which came at children and their parents from all sides – over the air, on the telly, in shop-window displays, in adverts and on hoardings. At least we could and, we believed, should, underline that without Christ there could be no Christmas, and that nothing dishonouring to him could have any possible relevance to Christmas.

Now, almost twenty years later, this truth is probably even more important. Often I hold a quiz for children who are new-comers in order to find out what, if anything, they know about Christianity. Less than half ever tell me what happened on the first Easter and, hard to believe as it may be, there are always two or three children who genuinely do not know what Christmas is about. On one memorable occasion I asked what a girl thought it meant to be 'a Christian'. She answered seriously, 'Not being a Brahmin.' They had 'done' comparative religion that year at her school.

That was the basic reason for our Family afternoon; and we decided on some sort of pageant or drama both as a means of drawing in parents (mums in particular like to see their children taking part) and as a supplementary teaching aid. We always started formally, with carols, prayer and a simple Bible reading by one or two of the older youngsters. We included one carol for tiny children who stood on the platform often too self-conscious to sing but holding up pictures to illustrate the verses while their harassed teachers sang. The summing up of the afternoon with the direct and plain message of Christmas came last, after the pageant. To begin with, this was a somewhat tentative affair. We avoided actual scenes of the nativity on principle, since they tend to take away from the reality and unique identity of this Baby. Our first pageant was as near as we ever got to

124

presenting these scenes, when we arranged a series of silent *tableaux* while various children each read out a verse from the Old Testament prophesying the birth of the Messiah at Bethlehem.

It coincided with the first year the Durham Buildings children were with us and is memorable for all of us who were involved. Every child had some sort of part, even if only one of the crowd coming to Bethlehem to be taxed. I had two trunks of old clothes, curtains, etc. and out of this everyone dressed up. On the eventful day, we had to get the children dressed before it was time for parents and adults to arrive. The trouble was that parents had to walk through the hall where the children were waiting, in order to get to the main hall. As time went on, everyone always being late in these parts, excitement mounted to fever pitch; children fought and rushed about and clothes came off. The little ones, clad as angels, were herded into the 'office' for safe custody with Brenda Mason, and the rest of us thankfully forgot them until a desperate message arrived from Brenda: 'For goodness sake begin soon, or all the angels' wings will have been ruined!'

Somehow or other we managed to get the children through to the main hall and to begin. It was very much a family occasion as the mums (and some dads) had brought babes in arms with them. There were a few older children and senior club members were peering through windows. Every now and again the door opened and everyone looked across at the newcomers, and as often as not called a greeting. The children, dressed up and sitting in front ready to 'go on', turned and waved at parents, who waved proudly back. There was an undercurrent of shuffling, babies crying, and whispering throughout. Some sort of silence fell when I introduced the afternoon. As a pageant it was a great success for everyone was an 'interested party' and had come to see their particular child – not to criticise the chaotic scenes. When it came to the travelling crowds arriving at Bethlehem I remember a horde of small urchins being let loose on one side of the platform and tearing across to the other, losing most of their clothes in the mad rush. The angels appeared, wings more or less intact, and fond parents thought they looked beautiful. The traditional carols filled the cold, lofty hall, ending with *Hark! The Herald Angels Sing*.

In other companies, the end of the service would have meant the congregation leaving. But not so here. Having had a struggle to get dinner over and to arrive, and now comfortably settled, no one showed any inclination to move. We rushed behind, put on kettles and emptied biscuit tins, and welcomed everyone to a cup of tea. In future we knew what to expect, and every year since then we have had tea ready after our Family afternoons.

After that first year we progressed to more ambitious productions. As far as I can now recall we only did one more fragmentary pageant before embarking on dramatic episodes from famous lives. The pageant's theme was 'How we got our English Bible', and its 'inspiration' came from the work I had done for the BBC programme which had been so important in my own life. When it came to our own pageant we simply picked out a few dramatic episodes from the unfolding drama, strung together by brief narrative when children displayed large pictures which they had spent weeks painting, to depict the Bible and people in different ages.

After that our performances included two of Bunyan's works. The first, predictably, was from *Pilgrim's Progress*. This was introduced by a tubby, serious little black boy as John Bunyan who sat on the platform, quill in hand, and linked the various scenes with his story. This child went through years of Sunday-school with us, and unlike so many who drifted away, has persevered in his profession to be a Christian in spite of the difficulties of life where he lives. He has since set his sights high – on becoming an international lawyer, no less.

The second story of Bunyan's which we chose was *The 'Holy War'*. We interpreted the travellers who arrive at the city Mansoul as Space-Men. This was very popular, and contained splendid scenes of fights and clashes. *Mary Jones and her Bible* adapted well into one of our plays and its lesson was plain to everyone. The child Mary Jones was played by Josie who was to remain with us regularly right through her childhood, and she has also become a Christian. Perhaps the most exciting of our productions was the story of John Newton, libertine, slave trader, then Christian minister and hymn writer. Jim built a magnificent ship for the sea and storm scenes, which 'sailors' pushed across the platform, and it fitted from side to side. This time it was John Newton, as an old man, who told the story as the play unfolded. We did a second performance of this production at the Home for Incurables where Rosemary and I visited every month, to take a most encouraging Bible study. I was nervous about how children would behave when they saw so many patients reclining or sitting in wheel-chairs. But I need not have worried. The patients loved seeing the young people and they, like most, were instinctively kind and quite uninhibited. Far from being put off by people in unusual twisted positions, they were most interested. They were also eager to push the wheel-chairs and we had to be watchful lest they began to race one another down the long corridors with their respective patients. All in all it was a good afternoon and one that John Newton, with his warm heart and many charitable works, would have delighted to share in.

One other production lives in my memory. This was an adaptation of the story of the Pilgrim Fathers and the voyage of the Mayflower. This too had scope for action and excitement, and thanks to Elizabeth Catherwood who donated rolls of black material, our Puritan men and women were convincing to look at — save for one original feature. In our production most of the leading Pilgrim Fathers were black (it happened that we had a number of bright, regular-attending, black boys in our older class that year), and the Indians whom they encountered on arrival in the New-World were boisterous little white boys.

Was all the bother and work these plays and pageants entailed worth while, and could they really be justified as part of our Sunday-school? I believe that they were, and that they can be. They did not oust the main Sunday-school lessons but were supplementary to them. They drew parents in to our Family Services and to hear their messages, and they were a means of teaching our restless children, many of whom were already opting out from the formal education system by truanting from school, and almost all of whom would have nothing to do with too formally structured a Sunday-school. More than that, many of the children tasted positive enjoyment and interest from stories of outstanding Christian men and women down the ages, and became aware of what the Bible had meant to them, and above all of the motivation and power they derived from knowing the Lord Jesus Christ.

We took care that over a number of weeks preceding our Family afternoon, we taught everyone the story which was being produced in detail and pointed out the important lessons we could all learn from it. But I believe that the lessons were actively helped, not hindered, by the acitivity of preparing costumes, painting scenes, and arranging a stage set which involved everyone in some way. We held a minimum of rehearsals since I did not want the production to be a witness to the producer's skill or otherwise in training up children to circus-like performances.

In any case, rehearsals were difficult to arrange. They had to take place before our evening clubs began, but children's ideas of time and day were erratic, and they had to have their teas when they got home from school. Sometimes too many turned up, having forgotten the days we had arranged for each group, but more often it was the other way round and crucial characters were missing. Yet on the day itself we learnt to expect everyody to arrive and their performances were nothing if not enthusiastic and often agreeably fresh and spontaneous.

6: 'Mods', 'Rockers' and the Rest

The advent of the Rockers brought us into contact with quite a different section of the youth scene. Up till now the youngsters we had known were more or less local, and we had established contact with their families. We had got to know quite a few of them well and were visitors in their homes. So they were not just 'kids' out of the blue: we had neighbourhood and family relationships. Also the older ones, who had already left school, were 'Mods' or at least inclined that way and not 'Rockers', an important difference in the early sixties. They thought of themselves as the aristocrats, the Rockers as the yobs. Their respective clothes underlined the distinctions as well as their hair-styles: exaggeratedly neat for the Mods, and uncombed long tangles for the Rockers. There were scooters for the Mods, bikes for the Rockers.

Most of the teenagers whom we knew already accepted the norms of the society they lived in, with its wholly materialistic standards, and were reconciled, though reluctantly, to the acceptance of work as a necessary evil for providing the money to spend on their status-symbols. True, they had days out, they fiddled what they could, some threw up their dead-end jobs with monotonous regularity but got others instead, while quite a few, with more responsible parents, were apprenticed in good trades. Their rebellion showed itself not so much in opting out from society in general as in trying to find an identity for themselves in the latest youth extravaganza. However, even this was not truly 'their own thing'. They were being skilfully manipulated and exploited by the many agencies that had seen a means of making money out of them. They bought outrageously expensive shoes and exaggeratedly cut suits. They used expensive after-shave before even a bristle had appeared on their chins, and shampoos for daily hair wash. They acquired scooters on hire-purchase as soon as possible. All their money went on trying to keep up with the latest trendy image under the illusion that this represented 'freedom', while they shied away from restraints and discipline. 'I packed me job in today' was a frequent remark. 'Why?' 'I wasn't goin' to be told what ter do' or 'it was borin'' or 'I didn't feel like it'. And, so far, there was always another job waiting in the dead-end selection, because employers liked fifteen- and sixteen-year-olds on low basic wages.

But the attitudes of the Rockers who burst in on us were somewhat different, as were our initial contacts with them. They came from further afield, though still in Wandsworth, and had no sense of neighbourliness with us. One ebullient gang liked to call itself *The Princes Head Mob*, that being the name of a pub that is a local landmark. One of its rowdy leaders now has a step-son who spends as much time on the farm as we will let him. The red-headed young giant with scarecrow's hat, high jack-boots, and belted jerkin who first led the Rockers in, styled himself King of Wandsworth! He came from the far side of Wandsworth Common, as did his second in command, a coloured youth known as 'The Mole'. Between them they led a motley, tattered crew whose rebellion against society, for one reason or another, had gone further than our youths. 'The Mole' (Maurice was his real name), was the exception. How he had mixed in with the others I do not know, except that it was while he was still at school. At that time there were only a few coloured children in the area, so that most probably he had been rejected and had found himself with the white 'drop-outs'. In himself he was very different from them. He had been brought up in the strict discipline of some West-Indian homes. His

parents had obviously tried to impose a rigid up-
bringing such as they had known themselves, but had
failed to understand the difficulties which faced their
family when they came in contact with children from a
different and more permissive way of life. The result for
Maurice was rebellion. But at the same time he was the
most self-controlled, self-disciplined youth we had come
across, and we soon realised that with him on our side,
we had nothing to worry about from the others. Dave,
the 'King', was a large, burly extrovert with tremendous
gusto and a loud voice. The 'Mole' was quiet, observant
and efficient; and when he asserted himself, it was he
whom the others followed, not Dave.

At the time they walked in on us they had been
amusing themselves wrecking trains in the sidings outside the Junction. But they were looking for pastures
new. I do not think they expected that we would accept
them. Our Mods certainly did not, and were upset. It
was understandable, for up till now the club had been
theirs, and they saw no reason why it should not remain
small and exclusive. On the other hand, I could not see
it that way. Once again we had to think through our
first principles. None of us had set out with the aim of
running a youth club. This had evolved, but our first
concern was still to show and tell people, whoever they
were, that the Gospel is for them. In that case, how
could we keep out our newcomers? I decided to pursue
our previous course of welcoming *anyone*, until their
behaviour was so dangerously anti-social that for the
sake of everyone else they had to go. So began a quite
new era at the club's 'senior' nights. It led to tensions;
some of the local youths drifted away for a while when
the Rockers were in the club, but they came in at other
times.

As for the original group of Rockers (for they were a
prelude to many more strangers arriving), we learnt a lot
through having them. Initially, they moved about in a
tight-knit, boisterous and aggressive gang. They arrived
together, stood together, played snooker together and

132

so on. But it was not long before we began to understand that the ties which bound them with one another were that each was, in his way, a 'reject' among others, and together they looked out on a hostile world. Their aggression was a defence mechanism to hide a pit of fear and insecurity, though there were some exceptions to this. Dave the 'King' for instance owed his position among them to just the opposite. He had no fears, no doubts, no scruples, and a conscience already so hard as to be almost non-existent. His boisterous sureness was a magnet to the weak ones, as well as to the few hard-liners who were like Dave.

It was not all sweetness having them in the club. On some evenings one or two would arrive in a foul mood, and this was contagious. At the back of these moods were purple hearts. It was the first time we had got to know a whole group who were looking to these for an escape and a kick, and when they arrived in that state there was a recklessness about them that could not be reasoned with, and it was impossible to get through to them. From them we first heard accounts of 'the horrors', and of nights spent on the Common under the influence of pills, shivering from those 'horrors' yet irresistably attracted to the kick. At these times billiard balls were sometimes hurled, and I began the practice of collecting balls from the pockets of the table and keeping them in my large bag. Now and again there would be a sudden brawl and occasionally the lights went out. When this happened the 'Mole' was useful in commanding order and restoring sense. He never failed and there was remarkably little trouble.

I suppose it sounds odd that we depended on the 'Mole' to control his gang and certain other key-lads to look after different groups rather than putting all the responsibility on the various Christian young men from the chapel, and elsewhere, who came to run the clubs with us. But the local lads were much more effective. We did not choose them out deliberately or try to train them up. They emerged from among the rest as having a potential for leadership, one way or another, and given the opportunity, they thrived on responsibility. With hindsight, I believe that it also helped that Rosemary and I were women. Our situation was quite different from the structured 'youth club' with members in their early teens, for whom competitive activities were important, and who needed a young male leader with whom they could relate. We were involved with large numbers of youths who had already opted out from organised clubs and most of whom were over fifteen when they first came to us. They were not going to take kindly to an authoritative male figure. In fact whenever someone came to help us who was very dominantly 'male', he immediately stirred up antagonism and a desire to get the better of him. On the other hand, a weak man was a disaster. But with us, the lads' attitudes were totally different. We were not prospective antagonists, but rather gave them a pleasing sense of superior strength; they felt they could afford to come to our help rather than fight us. Besides, most of them had known assertive mothers who ruled their households, and they accepted it as natural for me at times to lay down the law. Added to this was a factor which we gradually came to understand, that teenagers and younger children need *one* authoritative figure to focus on, not a number.

Much later we discovered that the fact of our continuing to allow those troublesome youths to come in, made the first chink in their armour. I remember the 'Mole' remarking one day, 'No one never cared about us before.' To us of course, they soon ceased to be a 'gang' and we grew to know them individually. It was common and pathetic to see these so-called tough youths come and show us cut fingers or bruises, and delight to have us take an interest. Some nights, too, it was hard to get rid of them. They would sit and talk and talk. By this time Faith had joined us for a few months. She was tiny, and very attractive. But her appearance of frailty was deceptive. She was a fully trained nurse,

134

quite capable of holding her own with these lads, who, not surprisingly, would try to prolong the discussions. We would explain what the Christian Gospel had to say, and invariably came up against the same astonishment that it had anything to say to 'bad' people. Surely, it was just a form of insurance for the 'good' and those 'upstairs' (in the middle classes). I remember when the 'Mole' came in to tell us that he could not go on living as he had been, and had decided to join the Army in order to get away. When he left we gave him a New Testament, wondering if he would be embarrassed or despise it. But it became a treasured possession, and for a long time he wrote to us and came to see us whenever he was on leave. Last time, with his potential for leadership developed, he was a sergeant, home on leave from Germany.

But that was some time ahead of those first months. The change in attitudes was so gradual as hardly to be marked, but the time came when we woke up to the fact that the 'gang' as such no longer existed. A few had gone off altogether, one or two were 'inside', but most of them still came round, though not in a tight-knit group any more. They came in singly, as *people* in their own right and having an identity of their own. Even the variation in clothes began to show this, and they were mixing with others in the club including even the Mods, until in the end they had ceased altogether to be 'that mob' and were part of the club.

All this did not happen in a vacuum. The grapevine had been busy and we began to realise how large a section of youngsters in these working-class areas were 'unattached' and wandering the streets. It was from these hordes that youths and girls arrived in ever increasing numbers until it was not unusual to have one hundred or more in our derelict hall.

Any evening when the senior club was open, you would know some time before you got outside. The building was by no means soundproof, and broken window panes did not help. The vaulted chapel

135

resounded with shouts, as a motley crowd, sometimes as many as forty at a time, played a wild game of 'football'. We had stacked pews against the walls, leaving a wide floor space which the boys had levelled. The goal area was the space between the pillars which supported the gallery, a highly dangerous position in which the wretched man 'in charge' in the hall usually found himself. Perched along the pews on either side were on-lookers, who now and again had to duck suddenly. A constant restless flow of people came in and out from the other hall, and every now and again, before the light switches were changed, all the lights would go out. When this happened an angry horde would erupt into the other hall looking for the culprit, who had probably rushed out of the main door and was halfway down the street. Meanwhile in the other hall, a game of snooker was going on with some difficulty, as people jostled and elbowed past in the confined space. On the whole, players disturbed like this were remarkably good tempered and only occasionally lifted their cues to whack at someone behind them. A more annoying interruption came from those who could not resist darting a hand out as they passed and trying to seize one of the billiard balls. I learnt to spot the danger signals, and either I or another helper would stay around that area. We also found that scoring for the players proved a better way of teaching boys to add up than the schools' maths lessons. But, with all these distractions, it was difficult to keep up a conversation with anyone who wanted either to tell you news, relate his problems, or just talk.

Immediately behind the billiard table stood a table-tennis table where, again, players were remarkably forbearing when people got in their way or trod on the ball. It was almost impossible for this not to happen, since both sides of the hall were crowded with restless youngsters who perched on cupboards, backs of chairs and on the counter which we had constructed with the help of John Mitrega. From behind this, one of the helpers, and it was usually Peggy, served crisps, sweets, and orange drinks. Peggy had arrived to do the secretarial work of the magazine and in the daytime she worked in the old building. But it was not long before she was helping in the evenings too, usually in the unenviable position behind the counter. Although quiet-voiced and mild-mannered Peg was indisputably mistress of the canteen, her ready sympathy resulted in the most unlikely ruffians relating their troubles to her as they perched beside her. What we should have done without her I do not know. All through the coming years of many changes, she remained dependable and imperturbable. Even now, when living far away with an elderly parent, she remains involved with what goes on, and is ready to help with some typing.

One of the most demanding jobs for Peggy, or whoever was behind the counter, was to be in charge of the record player. For some time we resisted appeals to have one. The trouble was that these youngsters were used to a background noise of pop tunes at home, at break time in school, and whenever they met in groups. We did not think that we would do any good to anyone by refusing to allow records in the club. Instead, we tried to impose some sort of critical standards. We agreed that we would supply a record player, and put the records on, provided they were not obscene or pornographic or otherwise undesirable, but *they* must bring their own records. *We* would also control the volume and would decide when the records should be played. There would be no records on Sundays, and we explained why this was a different day from the rest of the week. Surprisingly, most people were content with this arrangement, and saw the sense of having us in charge of their records. Even so, Peg had to be watchful lest fingers, stealthily feeling over the counter, turned up the volume.

High up on the wall behind the counter was a text which a friend had had mounted on wood for us when we first came to the chapel. Bold blue and silver letters proclaimed: *The Lord Reigneth*. It stayed there through all our experiences and when, later on, the new building was opened, it was already hung over the main club-room door. It is there today. Its original white background has an interesting mottled parchment effect, much admired by visitors, and I see no need to explain the various vicissitudes in the old club that brought about this pleasingly 'matured' appearance. All round the club walls hung the Ten Commandments, painted in huge lettering by the older boys and girls. Contrary to the idea that you must not mention law or authority or teach any basic standards or you will lose modern youth, these great placards always excited interest and discussion. They also showed up many of the children's intense ignorance, in spite of having compulsory RE lessons at school. One youth of about eighteen had been carefully examining the Commandments one evening. He turned to me: 'Yer wasn't 'alf askin' a lot when yer made them rules up. 'Ow did yer think of 'em all?'

In the various wall cupboards we kept magazine and 'office' equipment, but we had also to make room for a growing pile of club belongings. The bookshelves were filled with a gift of some fifty Bibles from boys whom we knew at one local school. The school had a new and unwanted issue of Bibles, and the boys demanded that they be given to us. When we arrived to collect them there was nothing to carry them in until the boys raided the kitchens and returned with fish boxes. Our gift, and the club hall, stank of fish for weeks afterwards!

We had also acquired piles and piles of crockery which had to be stored. This was a present from the owner of the fish stall in the market. We knew his son and most of his nephews. One day he invited us to the backyard where he kept his fish. He was in a strange fix. The man who kept the china stall in the market had, for some reason, lost his warehouse accommodation. Temporarily the fish stall owner had let him store his stuff in with the fish, but more and more boxes of china had been piled in, and finally the stall holder had

138

disappeared. The fish man asked if we would like as much of the china as we could move. We spent a back-breaking afternoon sorting out cracked junk form cups, saucers, plates, jugs, teapots, eggcups and the like, and repacking some two hundred of everything. They all smelt strongly of fish, and many had minor chips, but that fish outhouse was like Aladdin's cave to us and in future we had enough crockery for all our various activities.

Any stranger pushing open our club doors one weekday evening might well have thought the scene inside chaotic. But in fact the swirling crowds, the noise and general exuberance went on within certain bounds, and those were set by us. It was not easy to decide where to draw our lines. Our situation was obviously quite different from that of a youth club attached to a church and run as part of the church's weekly ministry. Thinking this through more carefully in recent years, I have not been convinced that an 'open' youth club can, or should, properly be run as part of the church's ordinary ministry, but rather that this is a type of work that individual Christians should go *out* from their churches to do, while keeping links with the church. In our case this had come about without our first thinking through the issues involved, and our headache was to decide how to channel what had already come into being.

This, I realised, depended on what our priorities were. If we put order and conventional behaviour first, then we would have to impose strict rules on the teenagers as they crossed our threshold: no smoking; no swearing; and a general conformity to 'established behaviour'. But in that case we should simply be giving them the impression that Christianity was what they had always suspected it to be, just a matter of 'don'ts' to spoil your enjoyment. We should have no further opportunity for explaining that this was not so, or for getting to know the real persons behind their flamboyant exteriors. For they would go and never come back. But if we were genuinely concerned about them as people, then surely this could not be the right way. The Lord Jesus Christ moved among very unsavoury types of people, and invariably looked beyond their exterior appearance to *the point of need within*. Surely we must not expect our teenagers to change their outward behaviour as they crossed our doorstep, but must allow them to come in, warts and all, and try to get through to them as individuals, making the Gospel our first priority, rather than the issue of not smoking cigarettes. Only then could we hope to show them that Christianity was not an outward veneer. Moreover, we could surely look back on our own lives and find that it was as we found and were filled with new aspirations, that old habits dropped away almost unnoticed by us. Should we not expect the same process among these teenagers?

All the same, we obviously had to have certain basic checks and standards of behaviour in the club. No one could remain in the club if he was an actual danger to other people, or if he forcibly prevented others from being able to use the place. I would not allow anyone to bring in drink or drugs, or try to influence youngsters to take drugs or any other harmful practice. No one could carry a weapon on them, but was to let me have it while he was in the club. If someone damaged the place, they had to help put it right. If they would not go when we closed for the night, then they would not be welcome next time.

Sunday was to be a different day altogether when there were no weeekday activities. As we put it to those who asked, there were six days out of seven for us to work and pursue our own interests and amusements; but God asks us to put one aside to give time to him. Surely this was the right thing to do.

On Sunday evenings as many as fifty 'older' youths and girls came in, so that in all we had three meetings during the day. Afternoons for the children; tea-time for the teenagers, most of whom we had known from the beginning, and which still included our first group. Then a pause, when we rushed off to Westminster Chapel, and back again to open up at eight o'clock. This could hardly be called a meeting in the usual sense. Bibles were out on tables, and everyone sat about on cupboards, tables or chairs. There was no formal opening, but there was a lesson from the Bible. From that, argument and discussion might develop according to the questions and demands that anyone had. There would usually be several talks going on at the same time, as our very few helpers drew groups round them. Other lads and girls opted out of the talk. Some picked up Bibles and 'Sunday' books; others drew and painted; the rest lolled about.

It is hard to know what the results of these evenings were. Sometimes it was very late and most people had left before the real problem exercising some lad came out. A few were thoughtful; but all had heard something, and there have been cases when years later we heard from young men that what had been said had come back to them.

Our constant trouble in those days was to give sufficient time to all the varied needs and problems that pressed in on us, to say nothing of the demands on time that publishing a magazine made. How it ever came out at all I do not know for no matter what we did, we always knew that half a dozen or more other things were waiting to be done. For instance, I could easily have spent most of my time trying to sort out the personal troubles of school-leavers and older lads and girls: job difficulties, boy-girl relationships, and quarrels at home, to say nothing of Court appearances. I would only write character references or appear in Court for a boy whom I knew well, whom I believed and could truthfully speak for. To do this every time I was asked would simply have discredited everything I said in the eyes of the Judges, and rightly so. All the same I did try to visit lads who were in custody, and to go regularly to

141

see those who had long prison sentences. I have spent considerable hours in the cattle-pen type of prison waiting-room, bunched up with a herd of other visitors.

While I was busy with older teenagers, the little children and their clubs needed our attention, and it was important for us all to get to know their families. Then those of us who could were to give time every week to regular visiting in the neighbourhood, for we were continually coming across lonely house-bound folk and others shut-in on themselves. Nor should we neglect the youngsters whom we had known from the beginning, and all the early teenage group. They too had problems and particularly required constructive outlets for their energies if they were to avoid the hazards of hanging about the streets and being tempted by the local 'Saturday sport' – nicking from Woolworths and the other department stores.

By putting the social and physical needs of these people beside our spiritual concern for them, it is not that we were changing our priorities. But living amongst them every day, we became acutely aware that their physical needs were not being met, and we questioned whether it was right to have them in on Sundays, and yet to do nothing more constructive during the week to help them develop their own potential in adolescence. We could not hide behind the undoubted truth that it was the parents' place to bring them up and encourage wholesome interests, nor could we fall back on the excuse that they had the opportunity for plenty of leisure activities if only they would stir themselves up and look for them. The trouble with the adolescents we knew was that their parents did not play much part in their lives, and that without background support and stimulus, they could not make the effort required. They were one remove further back in their development, and had first to be motivated to want to branch out for themselves and take up new interests.

Our first step towards providing more constructive physical activity to occupy Saturday afternoons was the

142

formation of a football team. It was also our first introduction to the cut-throat, deadly serious world of competitive football. We began by arranging a few friendly matches, but these were voted too tame. Several of the team always failed to turn up and there was no incentive to practise. As in any case we had no one competent to train them, the result was a shambles in which everyone did what was right in his own eyes, and quarrelled with everyone else. By common consent, before the next season we entered a team in a Saturday League. We still lacked a competent trainer, and young Christian men were not willing to give up their Saturday afternoons. This often left Rosemary to cope with collecting the team and taking them to the matches. As if this was not enough, she usually found herself the only woman 'manager', and in such an aggressively male-dominated sport she was duly looked down on by other club 'managers'. When, as soon happened, more boys asked if they could make up a second team, I was sometimes roped in to take and support them, and spent bitter winter afternoons stamping on the side-lines and yelling encouragement to terrier-like teams locked in fierce combat. Afterwards muddy, excited boys relived the whole game on their way home, and at long last, half asleep from the cold air, I could sit by my own fire with some hot buttered toast.

Football was to prove a mixed blessing, simply because it was so popular and roused such passions. Our lads were tough and determined, and it was not long before they were winning cups. The man who ran local football competitions was impressed, and offered to train them for us on a voluntary basis. After that, teams went from strength to strength and multiplied. The danger was that enthusiasm for football could easily take over as the expense of more important priorities, and might actually become counter-productive to our purposes.

Although the annual visit to Wales remained the red letter week of the club year, we took parties out whenever we could, with the same objective of broadening horizons and rousing new interest. One summer we even took six of the older lads to Switzerland for an eventful ten days in our gallant minibus. I see from old notes that the entire trip cost the boys sixteen pounds each. My great mistake was to attempt too much: with John Mitrega driving we travelled through France, along Lake Geneva, up and over precipitous mountain passes to the Italian frontier, and back by Interlaken and another long route through France. We were all exhausted by the time we arrived back at the club, but it had been a never-to-be-forgotten experience.

More than once we entered a team for the Rotary Club's public speaking competition! To our astonishment, we won the prize when one lad described his visit to Wales. We even had a Judo exhibition, but that was not so successful. The visiting experts performed in our cold, dusty hall, but there was not enough movement to hold the attention of our crowd. The only time I saw them take a close interest was when one of the onlookers got hold of a long wisp of straw and managed to tickle the toes of a luckless performer. I dare say there was betting on how long he could remain motionless.

We also had a fishing club. This was run by a very efficient lad who now has his own electrical business. He drew up strict rules and arranged where our 'fishermen' were to go, but we had to drive them. We used to leave the club at about four-thirty am. and I have memories of sitting for hours on cold, dark mornings, looking at the uninviting prospect of Felpham Quarry ponds.

Much more exciting were our 'Adventure Nights'. The idea was to challenge the energies of lads who would otherwise be breaking into old, boarded-up houses out of sheer boredom, or daring one another to senseless acts of vandalism. Before each event we

144

worked out an eight to ten mile cross-country course somewhere within twenty-five or thirty miles of the club. We arranged at least four check points along the route where adults would be waiting. Rosemary and I would tour round the course in a wide arc, and would call in at the check points from time to time. The boys had to compete in teams of four. Before they could go they had to learn elementary map and compass reading, and once again we called in Musette Majendie to teach us. On the night, everyone met at the club and we all drove to the starting point at about ten pm, or later if it was still light. I did have the sense to inform the local police what we would be doing, but looking back I am amazed that we dared do anything so risky as to let loose a bunch of semi-delinquents on a sleeping countryside, and that we had no trouble with any of them. The only time that officers in a patrolling police car had their suspicions roused was by one of our helpers. He was a young South African whom we had stationed at one of the check points, and he had a duffle bag slung over his shoulder containing a flask of coffee and sandwiches. Unknown to any of us, the spot where he was standing was beside a large poultry farm, and when the police car's headlights focussed on him the police naturally enough expected to find a few plump birds in the bag.

At long last, usually between four and five a.m., the first team would arrive at the finish where we were ready to dish out hot soup and sandwiches. It was probably another hour before the last weary boys straggled in. By then dawn had broken, and some of us had heard the dawn chorus from nearby woods. We piled into the minibus and cars, headed for home and a few short hours in bed. The boys would sleep all day, and at tea-time would come round to the club bright-eyed and eager to relive the story of the night, which invariably improved with the telling.

7: A Body on the Sofa

'You'd better come,' announced Rosemary, arriving one day as I struggled with magazine proofs in my 'office' at the old chapel. 'There's a body on the sofa at the "other house".'*

Sure enough, what was evidently a body lay covered, head and all, in a heap of blankets. At a shout, however, it stirred. A tousled head and startled eyes emerged.

'How did you get here?' I demanded.

'Through the window.' 'He' had come from another part of England. But London was his scene, he explained. Drifting in the cafés, his money gone, he had heard there was somewhere he would be allowed to sleep. He had not waited for formalities.

There was another body. The house had been left locked and empty earlier in the day. That evening when we went to look round it, I laughed as I walked into the sitting room: 'We'll just see there are no more bodies.' With that I pulled back a chair from against the wall — and there it was, swathed in blankets, the body of an unknown girl. She too stirred and roused. She was fifteen years old and had left home after a row. After she came to, however, she was at long last persuaded to return.

Another night, a beautiful blonde with an educated voice made an uninvited entry and, combing her tresses

*These and other scenes all took place in a largely derelict house, No 15 Plough Road, which Wandsworth Council had given us the use of while it was waiting to be demolished. It proved a great help in meeting the immediate needs of the ever-increasing number of homeless young people who turned up at the club.

imperturbably, chatted as if it was the most usual thing in the world to walk into someone's house in the middle of the night and plan to stay there. Similarly, the handsome young stranger who, at two am. that same night, rang the front door bell and came in with a charming smile and hand politely outstretched, also seemed to think that there was nothing unusual in calling at that hour to discuss his problems.

Then there was 'the Hippie', deported from the States, who arrived with a Court's request that he be given shelter. And so he came, all six foot three of him, with chestnut locks flowing over his shoulders, pastel clothing, gentle, dreamy ways and a marked disinclination for any type of work.

Or again, I think of two of that alarming throng of sleep-walkers, the 'barbiturate takers', whose days pass in a grey blur centring on their visits to collect a daily supply of tablets. These two were seventeen and eighteen years old, intelligent and physically well-built but would be sitting listless in a darkened room, with brilliant summer sunshine and everything in the world to live for – outside.

This increasing problem of homelessness among young people first came to our attention through youngsters whom we knew ourselves, who either had nowhere to go or who brought along one of their mates who was without anywhere to sleep. The most common reason was a row at home, often trivial to begin with, which had culminated in them either being turned out or walking out. Now they did not know where to go. Their mates could not help. They had no money. Could they stay at the club? This was obviously undesirable. But what could we do with them? We spent hours phoning up Hostels and Authorities, but while we could have placed tramps and old men, there seemed to be little available for the sixteen- to twenty-year-old age group. We were repeatedly told that there *was* in fact a real need for this sort of temporary accommodation. But that was not much help to us or the boys! Several times the need was so acute that we did allow someone to stay at the club, trusting him not to open the doors to all his mates or to walk off with our property. And our trust was never abused. But we needed somewhere more suitable for these homeless youngsters to sleep for two or three nights in order to give time for their troubles to be sorted out. That was usually long enough for tempers to cool down and for parents and boys to have second thoughts. It also gave us time to visit the homes and help the breach. If there was nowhere for them, we knew only too well that they would wander into sleazy all-night cafés and probably be led by those they met into thieving and breaking into property.

I had known Number 15 Plough Road, the house we had been allowed to use, for a long time as the home of one of our most regular Sunday-school families. The mother was Italian and had been ladies' maid to a tenant of one of the Grace and Favour apartments at Hampton Court Palace, until she looked out of the window one day and caught the eye of the window cleaner. In due course she exchanged high life at the Palace for Number 15 Plough Road. Her maisonnette consisted of two floors above an egg-packing factory, though where the eggs came from I never discovered. The toilet was out at the back on the ground floor, and the only tap in the house was upstairs in the kitchen. There was no bathroom. Somehow, that woman managed to bring up five children and to turn them out looking neat and tidy. She also kept the living-room and two bedrooms spotless. One day she dashed in to see me full of excitement. They were moving into a new maisonnette with all 'mod cons', and with enough bedrooms for all the family. What was happening to the old house? Oh, that would be left empty until the whole row of houses was demolished for the proposed new estate.

In response to my enquiries, the Council was not unwilling to allow us temporary use of Number 15. It might at least keep it from being vandalised. So we took it over. It was one of a row of old three-storeyed houses fronting on to Plough Road and with small backyards behind which was a little used church. The ground-floor consisted of a gaunt, cement-floored room (once the factory), out of which led a small room with back door and toilet. A flight of stairs led from the front room to the living quarters, which were still well painted and decorated. Above the landing ceiling on the top floor was a trap door, opening to a loft that ran the length of several houses.

We equipped the place with furniture, carpets and curtains which friends did not want. Then we were ready, except for the most important item: someone to live there and look after the 'visitors' and the place. It was clearly not everyone's cup of tea. It was Spartan, and rather frightening. I think that pioneer missionaries of old would not have been deterred by the challenge, but at the time we had 15 Plough Road on our hands there was a general preoccupation with raising standards of living ('improving the quality of life' it was called), and Christians were not immune from becoming engrossed by this. We did however have two men living at Number 15 for a long time. They both had problems of their own, but they readily helped us and looked after the place.

If Christians were not eager on the whole to live in such surroundings, others were. Youths came and went, and the place proved its worth. On occasions too we had couples who had been turned out from their own flats or rooms, usually for non-payment of rent, and needed somewhere desperately while they sorted things out. Only a few months ago a man came across the road to speak to me. He assumed I remembered him, but it was only when he spoke of Number 15 that I recalled him, his wife and their baby arriving on our doorstep one night. He now owns a smart little suburban house.

Once again the bush telegraph was busy and clients began arriving from all sorts of places, many without prior warning. Among these were drug-takers.

149

Obviously we were not geared to having them, but we usually kept them while we tried to find somewhere for them. Many had little intention of coming off drugs, and these simply moved on when they knew that we would not let them stay. Another type that posed problems were those 'on the run'. In these cases I usually allowed them to remain for one night, no more. But I did not take any steps to inform authorities, for all I had to go on was their word that they were in trouble, or my suspicions.

When we were left without any caretaker at Number 15, and had people staying there, Rosemary and I took sleeping bags and spent the night in one of the top rooms. We had no alarms, but if passers by saw the lights were on they were apt to bang on the door and ask to come in. We had long talks during those strange night-times.

When no one was staying in the house, we used to drive round after closing the club to see that everything was all right. I remember one night in particular. When we opened the street door on to blackness – the light was nowhere near the door – we thought that we heard a scuffle upstairs. Mice? I felt like asking Rosemary to go and see, but decided this would not do. Cautiously I made my way upstairs, with her close behind. There was no light on the stairs, but I had a small torch. As I shone it up the second flight, it revealed a blank void where the trap door should have been. At the same moment a relieved voice said, ''Allo Miss. We thought you was the Fuzz.' I shone the torch on the speaker and recognised him as someone whom I had heard a lot about – and nothing good – but had not met before. He had a companion lurking in the shadows. I told them that I would not have them breaking in and they must leave. They were quite amicable and we sat on the stairs and talked. But I would not let them stay for the night and after promising not to come back they disappeared through the trap door into the roof. We waited for some time and were on the point of going when there were loud bangs on the front door. The police were outside. They had seen our light on upstairs and had stopped to warn us. On no account should we open the door to two youths who might want to come in. They were dangerous and one might even kill. Later, we were to know that one well. He was a born leader, full of enterprise and able to take responsibility, but he came from a notoriously wild family and had to a large extent, like so many, brought himself up. In a war he would probably have won a medal, as it was he had few prospects except prison and more prison, unless the power of the Gospel changed him.

Unknown to us when we took over Number 15, the house was soon to have another and even more important use for us.

So far, in recounting something of our experiences in and round the old chapel building, nothing has been said about our tenure of it since the Strict Baptists first allowed us to use it. But matters had not stood still. The Strict Baptists had rightly been concerned about the future of their building. It needed considerable structural repair (this was the case before we began to use it) and in particular the roof required major work. But this would involve the Strict Baptists in great expense which could hardly be justified when the building was no longer used for meetings, and when there was no congregation. There was, however, one important consideration. The whole neighbourhood was designated for redevelopment, and this was to be carried out in phases. Everything hinged on when the phase which included the chapel would begin. If it took place soon, the Strict Baptists could hope to negotiate substantial compensation, which might go towards their work elsewhere. But if it was scheduled for a late stage then in all probability the roof would already have caved in, and they would be left with a ruin. The Strict Baptists had consultations with the Local Authority over a period, during which there were various changes of plan. But at last it appeared reasonably certain that the old building would not be taken over for demolition for a number of years yet. In view of this the Strict Baptists decided that, since the building was of use to us, they should offer it to us for a very modest sum of a few hundred pounds, and leave us to cope with any urgent repairs. At that date we had nothing like even a few hundred pounds. But the same week that the offer was made, we received a cheque for five hundred pounds. We took this as a seal that we should buy the building, and that somehow the responsibility for looking after it would be met.

Our next step after buying the building was to appoint Trustees who gave much time and thought to drawing up a Trust Deed, and the work was then registered as a Charity under the name, *Providence House Trust*. We had no assured income, but to date we had survived and had no debts. We believed that our needs would continue to be met. After all, was this not PROVIDENCE *House*? And so in truth it proved to be.

Not many months later the Council revised its previous decisions yet again, and we were informed that our building and the neighbourhood round it would be demolished very shortly! One of our Trustees, Paul Wilkinson, who has much experience of the ways of local councils, took over negotiations with the Local Authority. It was agreed that a site should be offered us on the new estate, but there remained the question of compensation for the old building. As I recall it, the law required the Authority to pay the cost of re-erecting a new building of similar size minus the cost that would be needed to put the old one back into first-class repair. Since there was not a sound floor-board, wall or roof beam, we were not very hopeful when a valuer from the Council came to inspect the premises. When we received his report we were dumbfounded to see that he suggested that the sum of twenty-two thousand pounds should be paid to us. This must have appeared unduly generous to the Authority, because we were informed that two more valuers were coming to see the chapel. On the day appointed it was cold and foggy, and there was confusion on the trains. One of the men never arrived at all. The other went over the chilly building and later we warmed him with hot coffee, while I tried to forget the disastrous state of the premises. But when we received his revised estimate it was for twenty-four thousand pounds, and this was the sum that we finally received.

Even in the late sixties, and with a site provided, twenty-four thousand pounds would only cover half the amount we needed for a new building. We had never publicly advertised any financial needs in the past, and we did not think that we should make any public appeal at the present time. But our Trustees and friends made the need known to personal acquaintances, and Fred Catherwood, one of the trustees, was particularly helpful. The afternoon that Mr Philip Henman, well known for his charitable bequests to many Christian causes, came to see us is unforgettable. We looked out of the main door and saw a dapper figure in a city suit picking his way along the uneven, dirty pavement with a bunch of flowers for us in one hand and brief case in the other. He gave us an exceedingly generous donation, and in fact we had received the total amount that we needed by the time the first brick of the new building was laid.

While these negotiations were in progress, we had confirmation that there would be no more changes in the Council's plans and that our immediate neighbour-hood was in fact about to be swept away. Several streets were evacuated, the inhabitants being moved to other districts; high galvanised iron fences were erected and the bulldozers moved in. From then on this was a recurring event, until *Providence House* stood alone in a scene of devastation that might have been mistaken for the onset of World War III. We were left intact for as long as possible because the Authorities appreciated that it would take many months before our new building could be completed, and that meanwhile we needed to carry on with the clubs as best we could. But it was a nightmare period. Only one access road ws left open to the chapel, and this ran between high fences to the front of the building which soon became a dust- or mud-bowl, according to the weather. Machinery for pile-driving foundations for the new blocks of flats came within a few feet of our building, and as the foundations were driven into the ground our walls were continually shaken. It was impossible to keep clouds of swirling dirt out from the building, and our telephone wires were constantly cut by passing machinery.

We struggled on for several months in this way. We had to bring all our old ladies to their weekly meeting in the van because it would not have been safe to let them walk through the ruts and rubble of our road. Neither could we let small children go home alone in the evenings, and on Sunday afternoons it was impossible to avoid dust and mud being brought inside on the children's shoes. As often as not bulldozers were at work on Sundays, and we held our classes to the accompaniment of throbs and bumps. One afternoon I had just begun to tell an Old Testament story to the whole Sunday-school, when the door burst open and Firemen, complete with helmets and gear, rushed in.

'You can't come in now,' I said, 'this is a Sunday-school.'

'Not for long it won't be,' retorted their leader. 'Come over 'ere, Lidy.' He took me to the side wall and I noticed a wisp of smoke. When I touched the wall it was hot. 'It's on fire outside,' the fireman told me. We abandoned Sunday-school and the children spent a fascinating afternoon watching the firemen.

Evening clubs were hardly less difficult to run. Mud and dirt came in with everyone. The sheer effort of reaching us was considerable, and one boy sighed as he came in: 'I 'as to climb four of them great fences, and go across I don't know 'ow many ditches to get 'ere.' He could of course have walked a quarter of a mile round and approached by the road, but what healthy lad would do that?

This ghastly state of affairs could not go on for very long, and we had urgently to decide what to do in the interim between moving out from the old building and the day when when the new would be ready for occupation. With some misgivings I arranged to have the use of the main ground floor hall of a local junior school on two evenings a week, in order to keep contact with the younger children and with those in their early teens. My misgivings were to be fully justified. We had to bring all our equipment with us each evening, and take it away again, and we had somehow to contain children in the one hall when there were four or five separate exits from it to other parts of the school. In addition, we had to guard the main entrance, or we should have had crowds of every age rushing in. As it was, those whom we kept out perched in rows on the long wall outside our hall and peered in, from time to time making catcalls.

We did not allow older teenagers into the school. Instead we opened up Number 15 Plough Road for them on two nights a week. In fact that house became vitally important to us in the interim months between our two buildings. We stored all our club, and some of the magazine, equipment there, as well as our Sunday-school things. We set out a small snooker table and darts board in the downstairs 'egg packing' room, and brought in a few tables and chairs. In order to liven the room up and give the illusion of warmth, several lads painted the walls a brilliant tangerine and we put in a wall heater. In spite of this, the draught whistled under doors and the cold concrete floor numbed our feet. But lads still came, also a few girls.

It was while we were using Number 15 as a club room that I acquired Hendrix. She was several months old, with shaggy grey-black coat and hair falling over her eyes. She had already had several homes before Roy and Les got her and the boys named her most inappropriately. But Roy's mother would not let him keep her.

155

Dogs were not allowed in the flats and she kept digging holes in their neighbour's garden. Every time Roy's mother gave her away, Hendrix found her way back. One day I went to visit the home and the puppy came and put her head on my knee, eyeing me soulfuly. 'My, she's taken a real fancy to you,' exclaimed Roy's mother hopefully. 'All right,' I said, 'I'll have her, if she'll come.' Hendrix jumped into the van and never showed any signs of homesickness, though she was delighted to come down to Number 15 with me and play with the boys. Now at the ripe old age of fourteen and a half she is lying in a shaggy tangle beside me as I write. She is still not too old, though, to chase one of our many cats or to scavenge on top of the muck-heap.

Sundays at Number 15 reminded me of *The Old Woman Who Lived in a Shoe*. The house was alive with children. Tinies met in the awful back room and in the egg-packing area. Girls occupied the front sitting-room, taught by Mrs Jenkins who bravely persevered in her stance in front of the fireplace in spite of rustlings in the chimney behind her. A younger girls' class was taught in the kitchen by Doris, a member of the *European Missionary Fellowship* who, much later, was to work full-time in the new club. I took the older boys class in one of the bedrooms at the top of the house, and the younger ones met in the back room with one of the other helpers. Rosemary drove van loads of children to and from the house.

The date for our final removal from the old building had been arranged for a day in August. But we decided to try to move everything out before we went on our annual camp to Wales early in the month. It was a hideous and protracted move, during which day after day we took van loads of our belongings up to Number 15. But at last, the day before we set out for Wales, we had completed the removal, two or three weeks ahead of our deadline. Three days later, while we were away and the chapel was locked and empty, the high roof fell in. Had we been there we could have suffered injuries, if

156

not fatalities, as well as losing our belongings. But the timing was perfect. We *had* been protected to the end. It was as if it had all been worked out for us.

This thought comforted me as I looked apprehensively to what lay ahead: a large new building on an entirely new estate peopled for the most part by strangers. How could we possibly manage? We had no assured income, and the new building would have to be properly maintained and looked after; we would need more helpers, and where would they come from? Now and again I would wake in the night, sweating, as I thought about the foolishness of such an undertaking. Had I been able to look into the future my fears would hardly have been allayed. But as yet I had no premonitions of what was to come: of the crowds of 'bother' boys and girls who would make their home with us; of the arrival in large numbers of more and more black youths and girls as the population of the new estates changed dramatically; of the rising tide of racial tensions, bitternesses and violence in the estates and the inevitable repercussions among black and white youths; of the crisis of identity for young black people and the alienation of so many of them from society in general. Nor could I see our involvement in all this or the steps that we should take in the immediate vicinity, or in extending our work further afield and embarking on a project whose name describes its aim: 'A Lung for the City'.

What I could do, however, was to look back over the past few years and take stock. How were we to account for all that had happened? We had come a long way in an unexpected direction since we had first arrived as strangers to the neighbourhood with the sole intention of using the old building to house a magazine. We had had few resources then and no equipment or expertise. Surely as we stepped out into the unknown and embarked on an entirely new chapter of events, we should take courage and go forward with some confidence, daring like Samuel to declare, 'Hitherto hath the Lord helped us'.